PATRICKE JOHNS HEINE

PERSONALITY AND
SOCIAL THEORY

ALLEN LANE THE PENGUIN PRESS

Editor: Ralph W. Heine

Copyright © Patricke Johns Heine, 1971

First published in the United States of America in 1971 by
Aldine Publishing Company, Chicago

Published in Great Britain in 1972

Allen Lane The Penguin Press
74 Grosvenor Street, London W 1

ISBN 0 7139 0335 X

Printed in Great Britain by
Clarke, Doble & Brendon Ltd, Plymouth
Set in Times Roman

73-160868

Contents

Foreword   vii
Preface   ix
Introduction   xi

PART I   INDIVIDUALITY

1   Early Social Psychology   3
2   Experimental Social Psychology   16
3   Interaction Theory   32

PART II   ROLES

4   Character and Society   39
5   Socialization   61
6   Role Analysis   87
7   Role and Self   133
8   Criticisms of Role Analysis   143

PART III   CHANGE

9   Change: Social and Individual   153

Conclusions   178
Appendix   185
Bibliography   191
Index   201

Foreword

I T is characteristic of members of a scientific discipline to pursue their interests as if they exist in splendid isolation from any other body of knowledge. Universities have fostered this conceit by departmentalizing the faculty and, thereby, adding organizational barriers to such weak ecumenical impulses as might exist.

Despite the occasional excitement generated by members of adjacent disciplines who meet at the border to discuss common interests, the situation in the social sciences has not changed substantially since they, one by one, escaped from the embrace of philosophers. Despite Lewin's repeated assertion decades ago that B = f (PE),* psychologists concerned with personality have managed to avoid coming to grips with E and sociologists have given little credence to P's role in social process.

In consequence, psychologists have an unenviable record in their attempts to demonstrate the predictive validity of their measures of personality, because individuals are remarkably responsive to their social milieu, while sociologists have found that both prediction and induction of social change often fail because individuals do not do what they are, theoretically, supposed to do.

As the author demonstrates, if the concept B = f (PE) is realized at all, it is in the area of 'social psychology'. Yet even in this area of convergence of interest, endeavours are not fully collaborative. Psychologists and sociologists each endorse their own brand of social psychology and, while there are increasing numbers of double-jointed professionals who are acceptable to both camps, their influence in the heartland of the two social sciences is not conspicuous.

Therefore, one goal in publishing this book is to expand

* Behaviour is a function of person and environment.

the interest of future psychologists and sociologists in a fruitful integration of the study of individual behaviour and the social milieu in which behaviour occurs. For example, major steps might be taken in solving the criterion problem in personality research if it were possible to adduce reliable and valid measures of role performance. On the other hand, some predictions based on sociological research might be sharpened if sampling were based on a respondent's subjective perception of his status, mobility, and of the opportunities and rewards available to him. The assessment specialist is dismayed when ascribed personality characteristics seem to lack durability across situations; the social planner is dismayed because significant numbers of individuals in a particular social category often behave in a manner seemingly contrary to their self-interest. Surely one constructive approach to the resolution of these dilemmas is a closer look at the problem of personality in sociology.

Psychologists are now venturing into the community with the view of studying (and intervening in) the effects on personality of the social environments in which individuals live, work, and play. Thus there is a clear need for a framework and a vocabulary for cogently examining the problem of the social experience in personality theory. Since it is doubtful whether any comprehensive and yet coherent review of this topic can be said to exist, perhaps this book will move some reader to undertake that difficult but necessary task.

RALPH W. HEINE

Preface

THE problem of personality, like many other borderline issues, falls within the province called social psychology. Presumably it is a problem neither to sociology (which functions at one level, it is said) nor to psychology (which allegedly functions at another). It is merely a problem when we try to harmonize the spheres. Then we recognize it as the only problem in social psychology, wonderfully disguised by the many shapes and forms its controversies have assumed over time. Here, therefore, the relation of the individual to the group – old territory to the social psychologist – is approached through social definitions of person and personality.

The distinctive sociological contributions to the field are usually proclaimed to be role theory, role analysis, and role research, and essentially this essay is about the rise and decline of that small edifice. Part I is a summary of the milieu in which it grew; Part II is a discussion of its theory and research; Part III is a review of critical developments that make role analysis something less than eternal in time and place, and something less than fully satisfying in social thought and theory.

The present text grew out of a briefer discussion, 'The Problem of Personality in Sociological Theory', published in Wepman and Heine, *Concepts of Personality* (1963). Now, as then, I am deeply grateful to the editor, Ralph Heine, for suggestions, criticisms and encouragement. To Robert Wesner of Aldine I should like to say special thanks for his reading of the manuscript and his intelligent guidance in certain matters of content and organization. Finally, I should like to add an appreciation of an old teacher whose influence was, as the saying goes, 'formative' – Hans H. Gerth of the University of Wisconsin.

Introduction

T H E R E has long been debate about 'self', 'person', or 'individuality' that we have come to recognize as a crisis of modern times. Since it is our fashion to call 'philosophic' problems that are either poorly formulated or inadequately resolved by empirical investigation, certain inherent difficulties that beset a would-be 'science of personality' may be considered philosophic. To label these as philosophic, logical, or empirical, however, hardly matters, for they may be expressed in any of these terms.

Let us begin with the last first. The exaltation of the individual and his individuality – religiously as individual soul, politically as individual citizen, economically as rational man, psychologically as unique person – has been accompanied, in our world, by a steady increase in mere numbers of people. Even if we regard these two historic happenings as fortuitously accompanying each other in time, we cannot avoid noting a certain disharmony between the rise of the individual and the enormous growth of modern populations. Very simply: large numbers of people stand as a denial to the singularity or significance of any one person. Hence from the beginning we might well ask the naïve question of where the individual comes in, what he counts for in a world steadily numbering more and more people, and what does 'being individual' signify? In the modern world, we know that numbers count: actuarial truths have supplanted knowledge, and probability statements have replaced scientific verities.

These are quantitative matters. Simple logical difficulties enter when we grant that the individual *qua* individual stands in opposition to such quantification and that, as an object of knowledge, he does not lend himself to the same procedures in quite the same way. What is different about the person?

We can know a great deal about him *as a person*, and it is

certainly a kind of knowledge – the knowledge, for example, we call personal acquaintance or a very different sort we call clinical insight – but neither one provides us with the basis for scientific information since its validity is limited to one. Therefore, paradoxically, we have to suggest that in order to have scientific knowledge about the individual we have to ignore him as an individual and forget, for the nonce, that he is a person at all. We busy ourselves with the most various aspects of person – likes and dislikes, sociability ratio, voting preference, racial attitude, ambition and aspiration. We acquire an enormous lot of knowledge – about particular behaviours, attitudes, have-done and would-do experiences – but we do so by setting aside the idea of the person and abstracting aspects of his behaviour that are quantified and quantifiable. Central tendencies are the only basis upon which any generalizations about personality rest. An exhaustive knowledge of a person gives us case history or biography from which hypotheses may be generated, but not a science of person or personality.

Science, then, and social change together contrive to derogate whatever intrinsic values we have learned to attach to individuality *per se*. In psychology the problem of individuality has often been construed as the measurement of individual differences with measurement as the predominant concern. But the bona fide personality theorist strives for much more than what can be measured. His claims and his interests are directed, we are told, to the 'whole person' – but who can measure that? Or his concern is with the similarities as well as the dissimilarities between people – a rather long detour from person and personality, but close indeed to social psychology. Scientific generalizations, we have said, inevitably derogate the individual because, in order to achieve these at all, we have to bypass the individual *qua* individual and concentrate on particular behaviours, attitudes, or experiences. Perhaps the first illusion to be surrendered is that the psychology of personality has, in practice, been concerned with the individual instead of bits and pieces of him.

We have alluded to the facts of social change that have

contributed to the relative insignificance of any given person while, in principle, individualism was applauded. Here the sociologist is less likely to emphasize the mere demographic facts than vast institutional changes. These changes have involved the uprooting of the individual from traditional organizations, his formal freedom within a new industrial order to go on alone, and, at the same time, political struggles for 'emancipation', for 'rights', for 'security' – all of which involved a ceaseless interplay between individual and collective aims, individual and collective action, individual and collective significance. Formally, in modern times, the individual was set free, yet individually he counted for little. He was (as it came to be phrased) part of a 'lonely crowd'; a surfeit of individuality made any kind of association or solidarity compellingly attractive. From this standpoint, individuality is not so much a blessing as a pathology (Durkheim called it *anomie*, in reference to the collapse of common binding norms); but blessing or not, it has issued in clear conflict between formal cultural emphasis on individuality and concrete social experiences that belied it. The Western world in modern times has known cults of 'genius', of 'self-expression', of 'self-realization'; more mundanely it has encouraged aggrandizement and achievement, the will to power and self-advancement. Yet in the face of objectively limited circumstances and requirements, only so much individuality is socially useful or necessary. A disproportionate amount may be variously seen as a crisis of individualism, a frustration of social opportunity or a problem of conformity. Superfluous individuality may be defined as failure or aberration, rebellion or eccentricity, but it is granted scant honour. Merton's typology of *anomie* is a reclassification of forms of social abnormality that takes account of all such forms of socially useless or disapproved individuality.

If there exist empirical and logical problems in the pursuit of personality, the most fundamental issue remains a quite different one – one that can hardly be resolved by ambitious attempts to define away differences in perspectives and interpretations through a consensus called behavioural science.

We may all agree that we have a common interest in human behaviour; we may go even further and concede that acceptable formulations for a 'science of behaviour' must, in quite narrow terms, be defined behaviouristically. To do so is merely to accentuate the problem of personality.

The human recalcitrance that is today sloganized as humanism in psychology and sociology gathers its strength not from the inadequacies of behaviourism or the insufficiencies of positivism – though these may be set forth – but from the moral affront each presents to our traditional conceptions of 'person'. Thus there is recurrently raised the basic philosophic question whether there can, in fact, be a science of person or personality in which the richness of subjective elaborations and the uniqueness of the individual human experience can find a place. An examination of what the personality psychologist actually does yields a rather different account than do his professed interests: far from being concerned with the 'unique person' or the 'study of the individual', his tasks have centred on sorting and testing procedures that group and arrange people either in accordance with prevailing typologies or by statistical distribution of particular traits. It would appear that only at the juncture of clinical and personality psychology (i.e. psychopathology) is the person, as such, focused upon.

The conjunction of clinical and personality psychology has accentuated and confounded the types of knowledge we use, on the one hand for 'knowing' a person and on the other for the scientific sorting of persons. According to our prejudices and perspectives, knowledge of the person may be either external or internal, but in contrast to the preoccupations of behaviourism, modern prejudices stemming from the clinical field tend to equate an exhaustive knowledge of the person with knowledge of the inner, hidden, and subjective. Hence knowledge of the person is likely to be equated with explorations of subjectivity. It is true that among the strongest of distinctions to be drawn in considering personality and its relevance for all social behaviour, and one that behaviourists have never satisfactorily answered, is the experience of self.

The 'illusion' of self is a favourite theme, often proclaimed by the same thorough-going social behaviourists who least question the reality of others. Yet what distinguishes person and personality from other objects is precisely the ability of the person to be an object to himself, to be, as we customarily say, a self-examining, self-reflective creature. The so-called problem of introspection, which the behaviourist dismisses as dangerous and unreliable evidence and which others insist upon regarding as a uniquely human capacity, has remained a focal point of dispute. Yet the human facility to reflect about others as we do ourselves and about ourselves as we do others is central to contemporary social psychology and serves to affirm the essential psychic and social continuity between self and society, person and others, or, as current formulations go, the inseparability of the terms 'personal' and 'interpersonal'.

In these new formulations the old kingdom of personality is lost, and the 'empirical person' remains to be defined in different ways and from different perspectives. Out of naïve social experience the person was, or could be argued to be, given to us; and so the self, too. Whichever way we regard it, whether with cynicism or delight, the 'illusion' of self, like person, comes upon the empirical self or person – there, like other objects, a physical embodiment with myriad attributes as well. Thus, we may see the person (and ourselves as well) in a great variety of settings, group or isolate; we perceive his shifting behaviours and postures, shapes and forms; and therefore we debate his existence because the very terms in which we define it usually depend on general and extra-individual concerns. Among these concerns, the psychology of personality has had its share in the dispersion of the person; and so, too, has sociology despite the fact that the person remains, in society and in life, the unit we perceive, understand or count. When we have been scientific we have had to forfeit notions of uniqueness, 'whole personality', and the like, and when we have delved into one person and his history we have had to forgo the usual claims of science.

Here we shall regard the person as a central point in social psychology and successive changes in conception of person as a point of departure for theories and researches in social psychology. The notion that boundaries of self and person are somehow fixed belongs to personality theory but not to social psychology. Here the highly bounded structure of psycho-analytic personality theory may be contrasted with the removal of all such boundaries from the personal self to the social territories within which the person functions (as in Goffman's social psychology). That sense of inner-being and privacy we have customarily appropriated as our own may be seen instead as the property of conventionally defined 'zones' or 'regions' that elicit or require or demand certain behaviours only in terms of time or place.

The shifting boundaries of inner and outer, private and public, subjective and objective behaviours suggest the insufficiencies of older doctrines. What one generation believed as belonging like private property to the innermost self, the next upholds for public scrutiny; what one era appraised as 'correct bearing' and prescribed as a code for conduct becomes mere 'front' or put-on to the next. External surface behaviours have been cultivated in other times and places precisely because they gave inner support, but such conceptions are hardly understandable today. In the absence of stable or uniform criteria, prescribed or given by tradition, inner needs, feelings or wishes acquire a validity regarded as totally irrelevant in the past. Correspondingly, duty or impersonal responsibility or objective requirements are often debunked as pious fraud.

We have no reason to doubt that new forms in social life may generally change the balance between public and private domain in subtle as well as obvious ways. But such change appears largely as a shift in content, depending on what is or is not taboo, seldom as an absolute decline in residue and reserve left to the individual. Sex, politics and religion may all – under quite different conditions of, say, Puritanism, despotism or theocracy – prove unable to be discussed and so driven underground or made private. These changes leave us no fixed boundaries upon which to anchor the self in comparing different epochs and different societies.

For objective reference we have had to depend on role analysis. Ironically, the very divisions role theory set out to mend in its unified theory of mind, self and society have rebounded in other forms. In America, its aspects of person have readily succumbed to specialization so that the exploration of the self was assimilated to psychological pursuits, the role structure to sociology, and in practice, its social behaviourism to the rather narrow exigencies of small group research.

But social psychology exists because we cannot identify psychology simply with the singular, the subjective, and 'inward view' and sociology with the social, the objective, and external view – contending that the one is concerned with the self (seen from the standpoint of the self) and the other with the person (seen from the standpoint of others). For sociologists the self is always social, but this view does not preclude interest in subjective responses to that self. But emphasis varies, and it is common to view as 'psychological' statements about individual motive and intention, and as 'sociological' statements about social function and purpose, with social psychology representing points of convergence between the two. So-called 'interaction' doctrines derive interpretations of personality and social system from a common theory of social action; the concept of person is emphatically 'social' and stands in contrast to the idea of person as a psycho-biological organism who happens to inhabit a thoroughly social environment. In these altogether unsettled formulations of the relation between the individual and society, the unsettling source will, from the standpoint of sociology, appear again and again as 'the problem of personality'; and, from the standpoint of psychology, the 'problem of the group'.

It is our purpose here to set forth the sociological side of contemporary social psychology – to examine its research, its literature, its critique, all of which, at one point or another, bear upon the 'problem of personality' or individuality.

INTRODUCTION

Person versus group, subjectivity versus objectivity, inner and outer man are oppositions that modern social psychology fell heir to but that, as a unified field, it could not use. The recasting of its key terms of analysis – strongly sociological through role theory and role analysis – has been so thoroughly absorbed that we no longer recognize it as peculiarly sociological. For a much longer time social psychology has grouped and ungrouped itself according to simple doctrines of individual versus group dominance so that 'group psychology' has remained a thoroughly ambiguous term. In Part I we review these old and lasting difficulties for an asocial social psychology. The apparent solutions to which role theory and role research seemed to point are presented in Part II. In turn, current difficulties and criticisms and discontent with role analysis are examined in Part III.

PART I

Individuality

I

Early Social Psychology

DESPITE its alleged youth, the field of social psychology grew in alliance with psychology itself; and despite its claims to a lofty and impartial application of the 'laws of psychology' to society, it was from the beginning embroiled in social and political issues. In this respect, the time, the place and the circumstances of its birth are virtually self-explanatory. Its origins with turn-of-the-century French thinkers who were highly vocal commentators, but not exactly psychologists, did not at once suggest a new breed. Moreover, they were not the first, but merely the more lasting and influential of writers to attempt to create a psychology that would 'explain' society. Their immediate worry was the crowd and the mob – hungry, riotous, revolutionary, or simply 'listening', the crowd was prone to unruliness and outlawry, but it was incalculably prone. George Rudé's (1965) critical appraisal of the crowd concept from a historical standpoint attacks the stereotyped conceptions of the crowd, including what is called crowd psychology. He eschews the view of the crowd as an 'abstract collectivity' whose social psychology is invariable in time and space, and he examines crowds as social movements, analysing their origin and composition, their programmes and demands. Rudé is a British historian, and what is most interesting about his study is his attempt to 'vivify' the historical crowd and make it live as social psychology. In America, recent sociologies of collective behaviour (such as Lang and Lang, 1961; Smelser, 1962) reflect

3

a similar concern. These writers, too, analyse crowd phenomena in terms of specific programmes and movements. They
look for the reasons behind apparently unreasoned behaviour,
and they dismiss the 'mysterious', the 'uncanny', and the
'psychopathic' explanations of old as no explanation at all.
The dynamics of tension, excitability, and enthusiasm are
'interaction processes' (they tell us) that can be related to
specific social settings without reference to the mysteries of
hypnotic or trance states, or unconscious or subliminal processes.

Such a view is an academic one without obviously enjoy-
ing esteem or popularity in academic places. If anything, the
old crowd psychology is reiterated with fresh fervour. Everyone knows there is a crowd psychology – a crowd mind, too.
It is different from yours, and from mine, presumably, though
all of us are in crowds every day. That difference requires
drawing distinctions, and crowd analysts, over the years, have
obliged by providing various classifications. But the taxonomy
of crowds is a large and boring task while the underlying
crowd psychology remains elementary and exciting. Usually
its assumptions are taken for granted so that it matters little
whether, like the author of *Great American Riots* (Headley,
1877), the description refers to:

1741 Negro slave riots or
1837 ('Starvation will always create a riot') or
1863 ('Draft called a despotic measure') or
1877 (the railroad riots that ushered in the labour movement) or

to recent riots in Detroit, Chicago, Cleveland, or elsewhere.
Nor does it seem to matter much whether the riot is a 'race
issue' or the 'politics of youth' enacted on campus after
campus as a new game called cops and students replaces, for
front-page news, the old one called cops and robbers. The
likenesses of crowds, not their differences, are emphasized. It
must be 'psychological'.

The concept 'crowd mind' did not improve the predictability of crowd behaviour but differentiated and named a

category, and in being so named, permanent censure was cast upon it. To this day, social psychology bears the doubtful distinction of seeking explanations for the inexplicable, rationalizing the irrational, and illuminating the dark intensities of a social order that appears neither very social nor very orderly.

If psychology first began (subsequently correcting its observations) with the idea of the sovereign individual – rational, controlled, in proud possession of various faculties – the first alterations to this view were made necessary by observations from the field of psychopathology and the second from the truths of crowd psychology, parallel but independent developments.

What immediately impresses us is the decisive and unquestioned antinomy between the psychology of the individual and the psychology of the group: the same body was of two minds, the one given to rationality – the other to its public collapse. How was this difference explained?

Crowd psychology was not a totally unrealistic appraisal of the social troubles of an era of great social change – it was merely one view of them. Today we may regard these historic movements as engines of social change and social betterment; to contemporaries they were merely dangerous, disorderly and disturbing.

Dangerous, disorderly and disturbing, so it was said, was the crowd mentality that set all those troubles in motion: 'half criminal', 'half savage', 'fickle' were the usual descriptive terms. Contrasts between individual psychology and behaviour and crowd psychology and behaviour systematically exalted the one and debased the other. And the 'laws of social psychology', which invoked a trio we still hear today (suggestion, contagion, imitation), made plausible the seemingly superficial and mechanical aspects of crowd behaviour. Moreover, the very language suggested that such behaviour spread like a communicable disease and, like other diseases, required public measures of control.

Le Bon (1841–1931), author of *The Crowd*, was a doctor of medicine who never practised medicine but tried many other things instead. He turned to world travel and anthropology, tinkered with photographic and mechanical apparatus and the invention of recording instruments, wrote a treatise on the training of horses, and spent some ten years of his life on research in physics alone (see Stoetzel, 1968). Social psychology was a late interest: *Psychologie des Foules* was published in 1895 (translated as *The Crowd* in 1896), and it was followed by 'psychologies' of socialism (1898) and of revolution (1912). Stoetzel tells us that Le Bon's work in social psychology had links with most of his earlier work, that, for example, 'When Le Bon dealt with pedagogy and politics, he carefully transposed to children and people what he had earlier learned about horses.' This may or may not be reassuring to the contemporary social psychologist; in any case, what is best known about Le Bon now, as well as what made him popular and famous then, is his description of the 'crowd man' and the 'crowd mind'. He was a great believer in the unconscious and in the place of nonrational factors in social life, and he saw in the crowd – all crowds – only emotionality. Moreover, he generously extended the concept of the crowd mind from electoral crowds to parliamentary bodies to juries – which may come as a surprise today to those who study juries in the interests of small group process.

When we speak of the early French social psychologists we mean a little company of men – not just Le Bon. His most eminent contemporary was, of course, Gabriel Tarde (1843–1904) who, as jurist, criminologist and social theorist, had followed a comparatively stable and mildly distinguished public career. Tarde's opus, the *Laws of Imitation* (1890), is mostly remembered by a series of clichés (suggestion, imitation and contagion) and is supposed to have inspired E. A. Ross's early *Social Psychology*. Tarde, too, wrote on crowds (*L'Opinion et la Foule*, 1910). S. Sighele, Italian, not French, but immediately translated and taken up, wrote on crowds and sects; his work on the crowd appeared in the same year as Le Bon's.

Altogether their 'psychology' was, as we have suggested, a now standard one. They were drawn to the mysteries of

6

hypnotism, the unconscious mind, and the power of suggestion and emotion. It is the enduring influence of these ideas that we would emphasize – how little, not how far, we have moved in any direction from them. According to these received ideas, the individual and the collective mentality were of a different order, and social life was imperilled by irrationality.

Whatever inferiority we still ascribe to group-mindedness seems to stem from these early conceptions of crowd psychology. Alongside real fear of the crowd, a moralistic bias on the side of the individual and his individualism was reinforced at the same time. It was less violence and volatility than the demoralization of the individual that was the real danger. This aspect of crowd enthusiasm had mystic and religious significance long before it was given either political or psychological interpretation in modern times. The persuasive influence of mere numbers was regarded as corrupting because it rendered the individual person impenitent or irresponsible as a mere number among numerous others. He was easily cajoled by a sense of false strength and false identification. In contrast, according to traditional ethics, no moral validity could be derived from others but must issue from a moral authority (God) or established institutions or a just order of things.

While we may be tempted to dismiss this crowd psychology, it has indeed cast long shadows over the subsequent course of social psychology. Freud's group psychology absorbed the self-evident truths of the crowd psychologists. As he pointed out in *Group Psychology and the Analysis of the Ego* (1921), he accepted Le Bon's description of the crowd (it fits in so well with our own psychology, he said) and only differed on the point that crowds displayed 'new characteristics' – not new at all but the return of the repressed. Ego and group psychology involved a common analysis of 'irrationality'. Moreover, collective psychology in America has in the past been identified with shifting, bizarre and 'irrational' group phenomena (Karpf, 1932; Smelser, 1962; Lang and Lang, 1961). Even today, the search for psychic propensities that either underlie or cut across social structures (which many see as the proper scope of social psychology) is possibly compelling only because there are many aspects of group life that simply do not fit the routines of psychology and sociology. These aspects emerge and re-emerge because they have not yet been successfully resolved but are still debated in terms either of the individual or of society. To this day a number of propositions dominate social psychology that are understandable only in the context of these early definitions. Among them are:

1. The ill-differentiated proposition that people behave differently together than when isolated;

2. That different 'psychological mechanisms' – facilitation, inhibition, suggestion and identification – can largely explain these differences;

3. That a major task of social psychology and its distinctive contribution in the laboratory is a 'demonstration' of differences between the individual and the group.

In fact, the numerous researches that differentiate individual and group performance permit no easy generalization; the psychological mechanisms used to explain such differences remain hypothetical; and the laboratory culture is itself a social situation within which variable settings and arrangements can be made without touching the problem of the purely individual and the purely social.

Generally the sociologist is prone to protest all three of the above propositions, but first the assumption that discontinuities between the individual and society can be easily isolated and scrutinized. For just as all contemporary sociology rests upon convictions of essentially communitarian bonds between men (institutional, organizational, sentimental) so, too, its exponents have viewed with suspicion all attempts to isolate the individual – to lift him up, or out or away from the social conditions that have made him a person – in order to prove his inveterate autonomy or subservience.

Thus, while it might be thought that social psychology should have had as its emphasis the continuity of the individual and the social, from the beginning the two were placed in antithesis, and it became habitual to counterpose the individual and the societal. This differentiation gave us experimental social psychology with its comparison groups: first the individual was tested or asked to perform alone; then he was exposed to a group situation and tested or performed once again. The average differences between his scores in the two situations were presumed to describe 'the influence of the group'. The factor 'social' was an additive factor and a qualifier. It corrected and modified the psychology of the individual and very often appeared to have been added in belated recognition of the fact that man was, after all, a social animal. Conversely, a 'psychology of social institutions' or social organization seen from the standpoint of its participants became a corrective to an 'over-socialized view' of man. This 'sociological' psychology tried to return to the experience of the person, to describe his attitudes and feelings. Its methods were those of the community study (participant observation) and the field investigation (interview), and it covered a wide range of social groups (gangs and clubs, professions and social classes) and a broad range of social settings (ghettos and slums, corporations and suburbs, geographic regions north and south). In all of these instances we learned to recognize the empirical individual and gradually to reconstitute a many-selved person.

However, even if, with William James, we grant that there are many selves, it is almost impossible for us to conceive of a self bereft of social attributes. The essentially social determination of self and individuality may also account for its surrounding illusions – particularly illusions of autonomy, supremacy and degrees of freedom. These are not altogether 'psychological' responses for, formally, in social and political life a person is defined as if he were indeed an autonomous person *vis-à-vis* others. Socially, politically and psychologically, the individual remains a basic unit of reference: socially, because we recognize the individual as the significant component of all group formations; politically, because the individual is formally an independent citizen; psychologically, because the experience of person (one's self and others) is an undeniable part of everyday life. Not one of these references can be separated from the fact of social existence.

Since the unalterable sociability of man is a biological as well as a sociological view, instinct doctrines were, for a long time, the 'natural' psycho-biological bridge connecting organic and superorganic views. Thus William James (1890, 1958, p. 393) considered man to have more instincts than other animals and the 'many more' instincts of man included predominantly social behaviours: imitation and emulation, rivalry and pugnacity, fear and sympathy, curiosity and love – James's list runs on for pages. He saw no 'material antagonism' between instinct and reason. Today, when popular Freudianism supposes instinct to be an irrational force restrained, with difficulty, by reason, we easily overlook the biological view of instinct to which many psychologists were indebted. In that view, instinct was not irrational; it was Nature's intelligence at work, and its sometimes cunning design fitted into the laws of nature and theories of adaptation and survival. William McDougall's influential and popular *Social Psychology* (1908) is virtually infamous today because of its instinct theory. His definition of instinct expanded to meet every social contingency and included the most diverse social tendencies – flight and fear, repulsion and disgust, curiosity and wonder, pugnacity and anger, parental and tender emotions, sympathy and suggestibility, imitation and play. The architecture of McDougall's social psychology was an orderly arrangement of the 'place' of instinct in the house of life – story by story and room by room. Early social psychology was represented by an abundance of instinct theories; only in their wake did social psychology become socialized as we know it today. What was withdrawn from the biological sphere was relocated in the social, for it had always been recognized that needs, motives, or intentions are not self-generative – they are carried by, not invented by each of us.

It would seem to be a commonplace observation that a person, any person, is separate, single and unique but at the same time enters into relations with others that modify his separateness, singleness and uniqueness. Hence the newer formulations of social psychology as the study of social inter-action have been much preferred as a way of sidestepping almost ancient issues. The aim was to avoid the separateness of individual and group and see both as aspects of a process. The act of relating to others, which we call interaction pro-cess, becomes, then, the meeting point for positions otherwise conceived in opposition – individual versus group, person versus society. Yet one way or another, many of the old con-troversies remain with us, and the formulation of the relation between individual and society remains complex, problematic and debatable.

Thus, the problem of conformity identifies another kind of groupism that captured attention long after group mind doctrines had been put to rest. Here we might well emphasize the fact that mere conformity can hardly be posed as a problem in sociology because it is, in principle, presupposed. Everywhere men conform – to different norms and standards, to be sure, but conform they do and without conformity there would be no social life. This unity of social life and the essential continuity of the individual and the social has, how-ever, been explained in different ways. We know that in the development of French sociology the so-called 'autonomy of the social' – i.e. the doctrine that social facts and processes had their own laws quite apart from the individuals who composed the society – nonetheless ended with the very apositivist notion of *conscience collective*, a consciousness that was, of course, different from all the individual conscious-nesses that made up a group but expressed the essential unity and conformity of the group.

While Durkheim is often chosen as the paradigm of sociolo-gical positivism, in doing so we have to overlook the way in which his thought came full circle to a kind of social psy-chology that was, with facility, translated as the 'group mind' of Anglo-Saxon countries. Durkheim's 'social reality' was odd in that, in the end, it appeared neither social nor real – it lay in the mind. The 'autonomy of the social' ended in the *con-science collective*, and the most elementary way of understanding the social lay apparently in psychic states induced by the mere fact of 'being together'. The abstract celebration of the social may be summarized in a key slogan found in the *Elementary Forms* (1915): 'Society is religion.' But it should not be taken as a key to all of sociology.

Needless to say, a scientific sociology could use only half of this doctrine. The social forms, institutions, and arrangements by which men live prevail quite apart from whether or not, at any time, men have willed them or are conscious of them; therefore, we can record and study behaviour from the standpoint of its social function and its part in social process without reference to subjectivity at all. Yet it is, at best, a one-sided account and, at worst, a constricted one. It gives us the familiar facts and data of sociology: the norms of church attendance as well as suicide rates, population data as well as technical inventions, fashion cycles as well as the public use of public libraries. There are also uniformities in social life that derive from the willed and the intended, such as residential choice or the planned career; and there are, additionally, by-products and uniform consequences that were not quite intended, such as the depressing economic effect of consumer saving ('under-consumption') or the crowdedness of the rush hour. All of these are significant facts of social life. If, generally, uniformities occur with little thought or reflection (rules and convention) and large processes (those we record as rates) can be measured just as we measure natural events, it permits us to set aside human intentions as interesting but irrelevant to our essential purposes. But having proclaimed this kind of 'positivism' and having established the objectivity of social life, we are not entitled to turn about and celebrate its often remarkable uniformity and predictability as reflecting another kind of mind called 'group mind' or 'spirit'. We know there is consensus. Can we infer from it a collective mentality?

Generally known as group mind theory, it is, in England and America, primarily associated with McDougall's (1920) social psychology, and its basic principle is more familiar and less outrageous than its bad name suggests. Basically, all that was proposed was that the group was more than and different from the individuals who composed it. Doubtful as the proposition is, it has lingered on under different names as group 'spirit' and 'ethos' and 'atmosphere', and the eminently respectable terms 'morale' and *'esprit de corps'* are close kin.

We have noted earlier that McDougall's *Social Psychology* of 1908 was applied instinct theory. His *Group Mind*, in 1920, proclaimed a new affiliation with a number of French writers, most of whom formed a kind of first cousinhood to the crowd psychologists. They were 'ethno-psychologists' and national character theorists, keen on race theory and strong on the 'superiority' of Anglo-Saxon and Teuton (Fouillée, Boutmy, Demolins were among them, as was Tarde). A hierarchy of races and nations and the notion of a primitive mentality (Lévy-Bruhl, 1923) was as natural to them as life itself. Their close but touchy relation to the crowd psychologists was because the description of the primitive mind bore some resemblance to that of the crowd mind. Both were 'inferior'; but in addition, Le Bon's notion of the 'uniformity' of the crowd mind sounded something like the 'collective representations' Lévy-Bruhl had called primitive.

By 1920, following the war, it might well be thought an insult to the mind of the 'primitive' to have it confused with the crowd mind. McDougall thought so too, for in the meantime he had discovered what was good about the collective representations that Lévy-Bruhl claimed for the primitive mentality: they endured as 'group spirit' and, far from disappearing from modern life, were quite necessary and indispensable for peace as well as war. They stood for sharing and participation. Hence, in the well-organized group, McDougall said, judgement and action were 'raised to a higher plane of effectiveness than is possible to the average member of the group'. Decidedly this was not the view of Le Bon or any other crowd psychologist; as patriots they seem to have been as silent about war as they had been vocal about revolution.

In McDougall's 'new' social psychology, the crowd mind was quelled and the group mind was extolled. These were, he argued, two different things. Then, after standing Lévy-Bruhl against Le Bon, McDougall proceeded to show how Lévy-Bruhl was also wrong. The collective representations that were supposed to be the feature of the primitive mind were not only present in modern life but indispensable to *all* social life. We recognize, of course, a voice we now identify with Durkheim, but apparently McDougall's acquaintance with Durkheim's work was scanty. In the *Group Mind* many French writers were, so to speak, engaged for conversation; but Durkheim is mentioned only once.

Probably we should not take lightly McDougall's war experience. He did not know soldiering, but he had interviewed soldiers. Medically trained, he had never practised medicine, but he did perform various psychological and psychiatric services during the First World War. As for his interest in things primitive, twice as a young man he had gone on anthropological expeditions. While much of his work had been in physiological psychology, and he came upon social psychology relatively late (as Boring's biographical sketch indicates), his interests had long been diversified. In any case, today, his *Group Mind* reads not like 'thoughts on war and death' but 'thoughts on war and life'. The group 'gives' and 'sustains' life, supports in the midst of hardship, creates endurance through solidarity, is the source of *esprit de corps* – in short, represents a high not a low point in social life. Nonetheless, to many, the 'group mind' was as comfortless as the 'crowd mind' and the two were easily confused. We cannot say that McDougall's brand of 'groupism' ever triumphed: it seems always to have been overcome by the older idea of the crowd mind. Even if it pointed to something 'real', it was not respectable; and it had been written not at the height of the war, as a 'morale' piece, but afterwards, in the long shadow of the war. Who needed, who could use it then?

The group mind was supposed to clinch the 'reality' of social groups for disbelieving psychologists and unregenerate individualists and, in its own way, to complete an analogy, not an identity, between individual and society. McDougall thus maintained that the group had 'its own life' and 'its own laws' and its own mentality. It most resembled Durkheim's *conscience collective* – with the difference that Durkheim took a dim view of the 'modern' form of social solidarity with its division of labour and its contractual obligations. McDougall's view of the group mind was altogether more simple: it included all the collective bonds that held men together, never minding what cast them asunder. He carefully distinguished all those conditions that set the collective mental life apart from the mere crowd. He praised collective 'deliberation, judgement, and action'. He saw good things in social life.

These divergent views on the power and significance of human gregariousness have proved remarkably durable: an arrogation of the principle of individuality, or its derogation and a heightened conviction of the inherent positive values of group life and group attachment. From philosophers to kings, from anarchists to statesmen, from artist as well as artisan, one or the other principle has been proclaimed and celebrated. A sample of slogans summarizes the case.

INDIVIDUAL	GROUP
Sovereign rational person	Solidarity
Human mastery	Mutual aid and cooperation
The active or reflective individual	The cohesive society
'L'état, c'est moi'- I am the State.	'Union makes us strong.'
'Cogito ergo sum'- I think, therefore I am.	'No man is an island unto himself.'
'I am the master of my fate, I am the captain of my soul.'	'All mankind shall be as brothers.'

Social psychology has, we might say, created its own vocabulary, set its own terms, and prolonged the discourse. If we hesitate to say that these debates have enriched the field, they have nonetheless enlivened it from one generation to the next, as we shall see.

2

Experimental Social Psychology

AMONG the earliest significant experiments in social psychology are those that demonstrate the effect of the group on the individual. Since few, if any, of us have ever lived any part of our lives apart from some kind of group, we might well assume that group effects are as diffuse as the air we breathe. Were it not for the clearcut assumptions of crowd psychology (crowds excite, cajole, and enthuse) and group mentality (the group levels or disrupts the higher intellectual functions of man), we should have narrow grounds for assuming that such differences either existed or were interesting or significant. Only specific interpretation lends content to the assertion that 'the group influences the individual': we know that groups influence, and the only significant questions for us are what groups and what kinds of influence.

Such assumptions concerning group influence are relatively recent. Conscientious awareness of man's dependence on social groups began with his emancipation from traditional groupings and his movement out of local settings away from village and family to industrial town and commercial centre. The disruption of these natural or traditional affiliations led to distinctively modern forms of organization (party, sect, union) that were bred in violence and opposition and only over a long time won the right to exist. The 'enthusiasm' of sects and the 'violence' of crowds was the earliest social psychology we knew, and, as we have suggested, it was a psychology of irrationality set against traditional conceptions of rational individual man. Above all, it was predicated on the apparent 'uniformity' of the crowd (or sect), its 'singleness' of mind, its ready convergence upon an idea or an act.

This elementary principle binds the new and old social psychology together. We may, therefore, recapitulate here the divergent interpretations that have been placed upon the most elementary 'fact' known to the social psychologist: *the tendency for a group to converge on a norm*. Such convergence, as we know, is obtained in apparently aimless situations, in amorphous groups, in experimental groups, in unorganized crowds; and social psychologists hit upon this objective observation as the purest instance of group psychology, for, of course, stable and organized groups evolve norms and rules with energy and purpose – and there is no mystery there at all. Still this basic fact of group psychology has, in the course of time, received such a wide array of interpretations that it proves a useful key to social psychology if not to social life, and we should attend to it.

'New psychological effects peculiar to the group situation' are produced, Muzafer Sherif once observed of his work; but how can one describe the peculiarity? Most 'group processes' cannot yet be stated psychologically without converting or reducing them to 'something that goes on in the mind of the individual'; but only the traces, not the process itself, could be measured. Those traces, usually interpreted as the power of the group over individual judgement, do not suggest that anything goes on in the mind of the individual at all. The 'convergence' is so automatic that it has created a psychological mechanism of its own but not a meaningful social psychology. It represents minimally social behaviour, and the hypotheses that have been proffered in explanation are reflecting pools of psychological controversy – imitation giving way to identification, the gregarious instinct superseded by a need for conformity, and the power of suggestion usurped by the requirements of congruity and dissonance reduction.

Let us briefly recapitulate the main experiments from their early conception.

1. First in the series are Floyd Allport's experiments, now loosely referred to as 'social facilitation'. The earliest of these researches was published as the 'Influence of the Group upon Association and Thought' in 1920, and a summary of the whole set can be found in Allport's text, *Social Psychology* (1924). Their history stems from comparable research done in Germany in the early 1900s. If we follow Allport's discussion of the problem, we find that his own term 'social facilitation' was intended to be both plain and precise. It was meant to tell us what happens to the individual in a group situation – sometimes the Europeans had called it suggestion, sometimes imitation, sometimes contagion. The terms had become obscure and garbled, and facilitation provided a seemingly neutral description. First, what caused the individual's performance to change in the presence of a group was not known; second, facilitation referred directly to the effects that were measured as individual responses.

The series of experiments were conducted at the Harvard Psychological Laboratory between the years 1916 and 1919. A variety of tasks was set: word, number and spatial tests were used; a reasoning test was added; and, finally, a judgement test. Thus, a range of mental functions was represented. Most were sufficiently routine that the criterion of 'quantitative output' was clear – for example, whether someone produced more word associations by himself or when tested in a group with others was easy enough to determine. The reasoning test was a qualitative one, however; it involved rating the thought and argument brought to an essay when written by the subject in isolation or in a group. On the routine tasks like the word-association test, sheer output was increased under group conditions. This increase was what came to be known as 'social facilitation'. The opposite appeared to be the case in the reasoning test: an individual thought best, it seems, in solitude, and abstract reasoning was not facilitated by the group. Finally, the judgement test (which involved judging odours) revealed another group effect: in the group situation, extreme individual judgements tended to be eliminated, and individual judgements veered toward the middle or average. That is what we today call the tendency for judgements, made in a group, to converge on a norm.

Discussions of experimental social psychology in America almost always begin with these early experiments of Floyd Allport. Besides the idea of social facilitation, however, he is well-known for his J-curve hypothesis; and, in addition to his social psychology text, his big works were *Institutional Behavior* (1933) and *Theories of Perception and the Concept of Structure* (1955).

2. The second important figure, as the texts show, is Muzafer Sherif. Sherif's experiments were done in the thirties, and his *Psychology of Social Norms* appeared in 1936. The original research was recorded as 'social factors in perception', and his choice of an old perceptual phenomenon (the autokinetic effect) as a neutral test against which personal responses could be measured has what is called the *gestalt* imprint. Again the experiments were done with students, and again the differences measured were those the individual reported when alone and when in a small group. The procedure was to record the 'movement' of a stationary light against a dark background, subjects stating how far the light seemed to move. Averages in the individual and the group situation were compared. The important fact, of course, was the difference between the two. Sherif found that the individual had one norm when tested alone, but that he tended to 'agree' with the group when in a group situation. This was the 'group norm'. It was like the third part of Allport's series listed above.

Sherif is probably best known for these early experiments, although his work did not end there. His *Outline of Social Psychology* first appeared in 1948, his work on *Reference Groups* in 1964, and *Social Interaction* in 1967.

3. Solomon Asch appears next in the chronology. His fame in social psychology also rests largely upon the series of experiments we are concerned with here. Earlier research had been in the field of personality and 'impressions of personality' (1946), which may account for his disposition to interpret his findings in individual terms. Widely reprinted in

summary form, the standard source for the discussion of Asch's research remains his own text, *Social Psychology* (1952).

The experiments were carried out over several years' time. Such sophisticated variations of the testing situation were introduced that comparisons with the earlier researches of Allport and Sherif do not carry us far. Asch's problem was something like the others, but it was also new. Again the research was done with students, but this time the task was different (it involved judging the length of lines), and, more important, a great variety of group arrangements was involved. The individual was tested alone. He was then exposed to various group situations: he might be in a situation where he had the choice of being alone but 'right' in his judgement while the majority of co-subjects delivered a 'wrong' judgement; he might, then, be given one or more 'confederates', so that he now had a choice of being 'right' with a minority but still 'wrong' according to the majority judgement. Asch also tried a number of these procedures in reverse. The most important aspect of the research was its variable group arrangements and especially the use of confederates to show that something like minority-group strength helped the individual to stand against the majority judgement and hold his own.

4. Richard Crutchfield completes the series. Best known for his co-authorship (with Krech and Ballachey) of a popular text in social psychology (1962), his research appeared in 1955 as 'Conformity and Character'. While not immediately obvious from the title, the research involved Floyd Allport's old problem – measuring 'group influence' – and, like Allport, Crutchfield tried different tasks and judgement. The experiments were diverse, the technology was elaborate, and this time a different subject population was drawn upon – professional and business men and college-trained women. Crutchfield used private booths (with control panels) and tested five subjects at a time. The impersonality of the situation was an important shift (the invisible majority was represented by the experimenter at the controls) but did not

diminish the 'group effect'. Different items were submitted for judgement, but whether the task was structured or unstructured, whether there was a correct answer or just one's own opinion to report, group influence seemed to prevail – always for some, often for most, rarely for a few. To interpret the findings, Crutchfield introduced personality measures after the testing. Prominent among these was the F-scale derived from *The Authoritarian Personality* (Adorno *et al.*, 1950). F-scale items are presumed to reflect the rigid, internalized authority of parents who demand obedience and conformity of their young. Attitudes concerning obedience, reverence for authority, pity or disdain of 'the weak' and admiration of 'the strong' become the signs of authoritarianism. Crutchfield found that his 'high conformers' also scored high on the F-scale and so could be linked to the authoritarian character of our time. Hence he wrote of conformity as if it were a character trait, not just a 'group influence'.

The above four persons represent the main body of 'group influence' research. Still, it was but the beginning of a controversy that was subsequently elaborated as the problem of conformity. It took many directions in the small group research of the fifties – mostly it came to be taken for granted, because so many of the studies were concerned with decision-making, participation, equilibrium process, and morale.

Issues and Influence of the Experimental Findings

For many years after Allport's initial report of comparison between the performance and judgements of individuals alone and in a group, the term 'social facilitation' figured prominently in social psychology. It was perhaps more influential as an idea than its supporting evidence justified, for even at that early stage a variety of qualifications accompanied it. Yet the notion that society stimulates, encourages or eases individual performance was an agreeable one, and it suggested, as a proper social psychology should, that the individual was neither submerged in the group nor was he aloof from its influence. But there has been little reluctance to part with its terms so that, while repeated references to it are found in basic texts, most of its happy but ambiguous associations have long since been dispersed in a host of researches relating specifically to morale, or output, or participatory role. Originally, of course, only part of the research indicated that groups really facilitated performance. It happened to be true on some tests, like the word association; it happened not to prove true on tests that involved judging comparative weights or pleasant and unpleasant odours. When, as in the latter instances, subjects tended to avoid extreme judgements, Allport described the effect of the group as a 'levelling' one. It was not uncommon to try to generalize from these experiments and maintain that in 'quantative' matters, the effect of the group was facilitating, that is to say beneficial, whereas in 'qualitative' tasks the performance of the solitary individual was superior, for he avoided the deplorably inaccurate group levelling effect.

We have suggested that the research was congenial to many prevalent ideas. It showed that sometimes subjects had quicker and more numerous responses when they directly contested others: but it also showed that sometimes the presence of others impaired the accuracy of individual judgement. Within the field of social psychology itself it was, as far as the question of individual versus group went, an even draw. It exalted neither; it was, in every way, a measured statement of findings; and it appeared to neutralize the issues involved at the same time as it pointed to further research.

This neutrality has remained the case. Generally speaking, group effects can be generalized as neither facilitating nor levelling; we still have to specify the conditions under which either the one effect or the other is obtained. The only significant generalization we can safely make is that almost invariably the presence of a group makes some measurable difference on the performance or behaviour of the individual as these contrasts have been set up in experimental situations (Walker and Heyns, 1962; Secord and Backman, 1964).

But our language can also be our undoing: we call increased output 'facilitative', but we hesitate to call 'facilitative' an apparent emotional input, investment, or dependence on the group that limits output in any way or impairs accuracy of judgement. These numerous effects – from sabotage to stereotype – have not served to enhance the group so much as to complete the dethronement of the abstract individual. In doing so the whole question of individualism has been recast in other terms.

Generally the levelling effect of the group experimental situation has risen to prominence over the years since Allport's work. In Sherif's experiments, which have already been briefly explained, a new terminology was created. He described the veering of the individual to group standards and demonstrated the 'group frame of reference' when he exposed an individual and a group (or alternatively, a group and then the individual) to a situation in which judgements were made of the illusory movement of light against a dark background. When Sherif discovered the domination of the 'group norm', he did not speak of the 'levelling effect' of the group on the individual, although the group effect of eliminating extreme judgements was similar to Allport's observations. Instead Sherif emphasized the 'unstructuredness' and the uncertainty inherent in the situation that could account either for group dominance or for psychological reliance. His interpretation has since passed into the social psychological literature supported by other empirical as well as laboratory data. According to this general interpretation, the individual neither necessarily 'yields' nor 'succumbs' to the group norm; he turns to it or depends on it because, in the absence of other criteria, it provides a guide and a standard. Here the hazards of interpretation rather than the often alleged artifice of experimental situations point to unsolved difficulties. How is its circularity to be escaped? The individual gives way to the group, but he is also part of that group; no dominance pattern is established but an average to which each contributes, wittingly or unwittingly. Consensus is acknowledged on all sides, but the interpretation of it has so far successfully resisted either clear 'psychological' or 'sociological' resolution.

We may wonder, then, how this undeniable group influence that Sherif stated in the seemingly neutral language of the 'group frame of reference' came to be refashioned once again. The answer seems to lie in the fact that his 'psychology of social norms' undid an old balance between the principles of 'the individual' and of 'the social'. Apparently establishing 'group dominance', it put in jeopardy the principle of individuality as 'deviation' from group norm. Thus when Asch recast the problem once again, he did so in terms that directly evolved into our contemporary language of conformity. He stated his various researches as investigations into the 'conditions of *independence of* and *submission to* group pressure'. The power of the group is acknowledged and the question becomes: who yields? who resists?

Perhaps the most interesting aspect of these experiments from a strictly sociological standpoint is that the results appear to have followed a normal distribution. This fact is seldom attended, and in the interpretation of results it is the question of individuality and individual differences that is rather dramatically focused upon. 'One fourth of the critical subjects were completely independent; at the other extreme one third of the group displaced the estimates toward the majority in one half or more of the trials' (Asch, in Cartwright and Zander, 1968). In between was the uncertain and shifting majority. In their way, of course, Asch's experiments exaggerated what Sherif had already shown, for the task he presented his subjects involved a 'right' and a 'wrong' answer, and swinging with the group was wrong. Sherif's interpretation had emphasized unstructuredness and uncertainty; Asch's emphasized independence and yielding. Asch's emphasis permitted articulating the whole problem in strictly psychological terms of 'character structure'. 'The presence of pronounced individual differences points to the important role of personality factors, of factors connected with the individual's character structure,' Asch wrote (ibid.).

There has been occasional tendency to modify the somewhat dramatic confrontation of individual versus group, or to emphasize as Deutsch and Gerard did (in Cartwright and

Zander, 1968) that normative social influence internalized helps 'make an individual be an individual'. They distinguished between 'normative' and 'informational' social influence and sought to create experimental situations indicating the strength of normative influence, for it was their contention that the earlier experiments showed only the individual turning to the group for information and confirmation. Other variations in this research have included the finding that attitudes of students changed significantly only where the students were acquainted with one another and clear personal advantage could be obtained (Lambert and Lambert, 1964) or, somewhat similarly, that conformity changed with group membership so that degree of conformity depends on wanting or not wanting to be accepted into various groups (Walker and Heyns, 1962). But on the whole, the greatest consequent interest came to centre on the question of conformity and character, and it is in this context that the original definition of the 'group frame of reference' was converted into 'the problem of conformity'. Conformity gradually changed from an objective social fact to a psychological problem and so, presumably, to a characterologic issue. The culmination of these changes is found in Crutchfield's research, which was briefly discussed above. His research converted a distribution of responses (similar to Asch's, though Asch found that these varied with the presence or absence of 'confederates') into character depictions by concentrating on the extremes for character analysis. By a variety of personality assessments the 'conforming personality' – not neurotic but rather rigid, moralistic, and authoritarian – could be differentiated from the nonconformist who, it was said, exhibited greater freedom, self-assertiveness and independence.

Incidentally, while Crutchfield claimed a correspondence between the authoritarian personality and conformity, kindred formulations had already been drawn from the area of 'persuasibility' experiments (Hovland, Janis and Kelley, 1953). Here, the 'unpersuasible' person had been described in quite as unflattering terms as one who is 'hostile, anxious, withdrawn, and resistant'. The personality of those in the middle (though largely 'conformist' and 'persuasible') has not been scrutinized in the same way.

What are the difficulties of these propositions and what kinds of criticism have sociologists made of them? We have retraced what can almost be called the classic issue in social psychology, because in many ways it conveniently exaggerates the whole problem of personality with its accompanying dreams of individualism and autonomy. Just as in Hamlet's soliloquy existence is brought to issue, so here is social existence. Yet to conform or not to conform is scarcely ever a question in real life, but a condition of it. Thus, whether we do or do not ally ourselves with the majority in any given situation illuminates neither character nor conformity generally. We may reasonably suppose that, while certain types of conformity may be related to psychological character types, conformity as such cannot be. But here the difficulties of the assumptions are compounded by the method of 'proof'. 'Character' was not introduced into the original design of the study, but imposed in the interpretation of results. In point of design alone we might wish for more careful comparisons and controls or we might see as better procedure exposing different 'character types' to a variety of situations. We do not wish to enter here the many reservations that have come to be attached to the F-scale, but of all instruments it is perhaps most social-psychological and least characterological. Hence the sociologist is likely to protest that whether we use a paper-pencil test of submissiveness (called the authoritarian personality) or a situational test (called conformity), we are measuring the same thing – but not showing the relations between character and conformity.

1. Sometimes character changes with the situation: we are conformist in some areas, not in others. 'Public conformity – secret vice' is perhaps its most dramatic instance; the 'lost weekends' of the public official or career-man, the private distempers or depressions of the public performer. More ordinary examples include the way we behave and are expected to behave in formal as contrasted to informal situations, at school and at work as against at home and at play.

2. Sometimes the situation changes our character: we dissemble real feeling or judgement; we 'give in'. This occurs in common social situations where we learn to keep our opinions to ourselves or where, to maintain harmony, we avoid argument as if to say, 'Oh, all right, have it your way.' Going along with the crowd largely involves this kind of congeniality and is often called 'characterless conformity'.

3. Sometimes character is simply irrelevant: wholly extraneous factors from physiological ones to impulsive decision, apparently without motive, determine our behaviour. The 'biological clock' accounts for much convergent behaviour – being hungry at certain hours or growing fatigued after periods of work are examples. The impulse to go barefoot in the spring or jump in for a swim when we see a pool of water happily outlasts childhood, but has little relevance to character.

In this brief history, what is most disconcerting is the shift of focus from social conformity to psychological conformity. We have traced here the gradual evolution of interpretation of minimal group process from 'group influence' to 'frame of reference' and from frame of reference to 'individual yielding and submission' and, finally, to 'conformist character'.

'Convergence on a norm', as it has been induced in the experimental situation, may represent minimal social process, but apparently provides no key to that process. The research tells us that people behave or perform differently as individuals than they do in a group; and it shows us how individual responses (whether judging length of lines or producing word associations) can be averaged to arrive at a figure we then call a 'norm for the group'; but it does not explain what has happened. It has, therefore, proved amenable to a kind of mysticism of 'group process' (influence, dominance, structure) and to vague psychological effects consequent, presumably, simply to people being together, or it ends by telling us that people conform because they are characterologically conformist.

In reviewing these old issues in social psychology, we may well ask: Are not researches purporting to show 'the effect of the group on the individual', or, conversely, the 'effect of the individual on the group', an embarrassing anachronism? Do they not confirm our submission to the sinister and obscure power of the group over the individual, or the opposite, the ambition to exalt to heroic proportion the individual who resists or triumphs over that power? The assimilation of these researches to sociology proper has been various.

Sherif felt convinced that he had discovered in the 'group frame of reference' the very foundation of social life, the 'psychological basis of established norms, such as stereotypes, fashions, conventions, customs'. But the fact is, we do not know why such uniformities occur though we have accumulated, over the years, a reservoir of hypothetical explanations. Imitation? Suggestion? Unconscious identification? A need for conformity? A strain for congruity or consistency? The parallels to be drawn to real social life are difficult, for group life structures for us, its norms and standards are what we live by, and far from lacking a frame of reference, the neonate from the beginning has it forced upon him. He learns.

Thus the experiments show greater kinship to the crowd behaviours and crowd influences that the early social psychologists focused on. They point, of course, to 'group phenomena' that to this day are poorly understood. For the sociologist they represent marginal data: quasi-automatic, near-reflexive behaviours and responses that indicate the influence of others often without conscious awareness or orientation at all. If we hold to strict definitions of interaction we may, in fact, reject their definition as 'social' behaviour at all, or we may bracket it as 'borderline'.* But whether so defined or not, comparability is found not in those large areas of structured behaviour we call convention, custom and usage, but in those relatively unstructured spheres of social life where the individual – many feel, increasingly today – is asked to

* For example, Max Weber, wrestling with similar problems, said he did not 'propose to call action "social" when it is merely the effect on the individual of a crowd as such'; nor that 'mere imitation of the action of others . . . be considered a case of specifically social action if it is purely reactive so that there is no orientation to the actor imitated'. See *Theory of Social and Economic Organization* (trans. T. Parsons), Collier-Macmillan, 1957.

make a choice without knowing how to make it. In short, when still found useful, these researches have been appropriated by new 'mass psychologies' – those that purport to measure 'influence' and describe 'influentials' whose vague authority has supplanted the traditions of yesteryear.

Modern social life, it has then been argued, has created more and more options that engender spurious consensus and encourage the so-called 'group frame of reference'. Advertising abounds in examples of the creation of meaningless choice; or again, citizens are repeatedly asked to exercise political intelligence in the absence of knowledge of either issues or candidates so that dependence on 'group' judgement has come to be inevitable.* Uncertainty and the need for 'reference' have, therefore, been viewed as the key to the working out of this principle in social life.

The late recasting of these researches as conformity experiments reflects contemporary concerns just as, in their own fashion, crowd psychologies did. Perhaps we live in an 'age of conformity' as the old social psychologists lived in an 'age of crowds'; in both cases, concern has been invigorated by political anxiety. That modern life has created the conditions for new 'frames of reference' without, at the same time, producing affiliations that might give meaning and direction to individual choice has led to the conclusion that individual choices are often made haphazardly and obscurely. Here, obscurity may stand for something 'heard about' or what most people are 'said to do'. The hidden, the subliminal, the vaguely persuasive have, in turn, been converted to nameless, unseen and unlocatable powers in the economic and political market-place. The new interpreters of the 'group frame of reference' therefore deplore the possibilities it presents for manipulation and deliberate management. But those sociologists most likely to accept its relevance as a

* Thus the clear relevance of Sherif's findings to voting behaviour has been argued by Elihu Katz and Paul Lazarsfeld in *Personal Influence* (1955), p. 56. We may be reminded here of the enormous literature of this period emanating from the concept of the reference group – i.e. the influence of groups to which one does not belong.

principle of social life ultimately insist upon seeing 'structure' behind the apparently 'unstructured'.

The popular sociology of 'conformity' had rather different sources; yet it, too, came to converge upon the character principle. The psychology of modern mass movements gave us the submissive conformity of the 'little man, what now' variety, followed by the 'togetherness' conformity of organization man (Whyte) and the 'other-directed' tyranny of the peer group (Riesman), as well as a quite various assortment of political theories of apathy, depoliticalization and alienation. The social types depicted bore little resemblance to psychological types *per se*, but the confusion of the two was generous so that, again, conformity appeared to be a 'psychological problem' and a peculiarly modern malady.

The inclination to locate the malaise of the times in the 'psychology of modern man' has typically centred upon the equation of anxiety and conformity and authoritarianism. Very often its specific linkage to the social order is lost or overlooked. Sociologically speaking, if there is indeed a crisis of individuality or a problem of conformity, our task lies not in decrying the relative infrequency of individualists or the conspicuous lack of autonomous behaviours, but of locating changes in social structure that plausibly account for them. So many symptoms should, logically, have their counterpart in social analysis. Such analysis, in fact, had been the method of the old sociologists, whose preachments had acquired, for many, the aura of prophecy: it was change in society itself that had conduced helpless forms of individualization (Durkheim's *anomie*) and cast the person out as a stranger and afraid (Marx's *alienation*) – with the difference, of course, that it was assuredly a world of man's own making. Durkheim discerned *anomie* not from considering the unhappiness of men but by observing the collapse of norms and rules and solidary ties; for Marx, alienation was a part of social reality, a way of 'being' in a class-divided, exchange-bound world in which men were experienced as things and things as strange and monstrous powers. Today these ideas have been preserved for us, not as deeply embedded aspects of social life, but as psychological states of 'disengagement' (the aged), 'disaffection' (youth), or disenchantment (almost anybody). Converted into psychological measures of discontent, they stand alongside other types of personality profiles as a set of values or attitudes toward society at large. They are not so much a social psychology as a psychology of 'asociality'.

In these many transformations, it is not the fusion of the social and the psychological that concerns us, but the steady widening and polarization of the individual and society. As a consequence, if we ask 'Who are the disaffected?' numerous social groups (the young, the old, the ill, the disadvantaged, the criminal) may be named as islands of discontent and isolation from the mainstream, their *de facto* functional disconnection actually obscured by the elusive and often emotive language of 'alienation' and *'anomie'*.*

We have commented earlier that social psychology was established on premises that set the individual apart from society, and therefore the very existence of society was a problem. How was society possible? Why did the individual surrender to society's aims and purposes and power? Was the group a reality? In supplying answers to these questions, crowd psychologists and later group mind theorists explained the existence of society in terms of psychic effects over and above the individual minds that composed it. Experimentalists either accepted the emergent group norm as their social reality or fell back on behavioural descriptions of contagion, imitation, or facilitation. New characterologists hypothesized the 'social character' and found unity in traits common to all the individuals in a group. There was, however, still another way. It was called interaction theory, and in social psychology its influence came to be considerable.

* The literature has, by now, become enormous. A relatively early and theoretical discussion is Fritz Pappenheim's *Alienation of Modern Man* (1959). Erich Fromm's *Man for Himself* (1949) and *The Sane Society* (1956), as well as Herbert Marcuse's *Reason and Revolution* (1954), are standard. Recent critical discussions may be found in J. Horton, 'The Dehumanization of Anomie and Alienation' and in I. S. Kon, 'Concept of Alienation in Modern Sociology', *Social Research*, 1967, 34, pp. 507–28.

3

Interaction Theory

THE aim (and it was an ambitious one) of interaction theory from the beginning was to avoid the old opposition of individual versus group. Its solution was to be 'dialectic'; a unity of opposites was to be sought in a basic process that brought together both the principle of 'the individual' and the principle of 'the social'. That process is known simply as *interaction*, and because man is a social creature, it characterizes human life from beginning to end. The group (so it is said) is built out of inter-individual actions of varying complexity; the individual is the product of interactions with significant others in his environment.

The basic theory is often called social behaviourism and derives from George Herbert Mead. Mead (1863–1931) was neither a sociologist nor a psychologist but a philosopher, among the most important that American pragmatism has produced. His work, published posthumously, includes *Mind, Self and Society*, *Philosophy of the Act*, and *Movements of Thought in the Nineteenth Century*. Social psychology has borrowed heavily from the first of these books. It is the main source for the theory of social learning through role-taking, as well as the definitions of self and society. This social psychology sociologists commonly adopt as 'their own'.

But the key terms of interaction theory – interaction, reciprocity, and role – have become so standard as to have lost their original connection. Interaction is essentially the behaviourist S-R formula; as 'social behaviourism', however, it is an open, continuous process in which 'my' response to 'your' stimulus becomes, in turn, a stimulus to which 'you' respond. An interaction can be as brief and as terse as the exchange of formal greetings or it can be as prolonged as a kinship relation; it can refer to large groups (a performer and his audience) or to small ones (a t-group), to spatially distant relationships (personal correspondence) or proximate ones (room mates). Reciprocity refers to mutuality and sharing that come about through taking one's own part (S) and taking the part of others, too, in responding to them (R). There is a constant shifting of roles, of one's position, in the S-R exchange; it is in this way that common symbols come to be used and common meanings are achieved.

We can see at once how agreeable such a theory was to sociologists. If it did not precisely begin with the group it did begin with a principle that instantly clarified the sociability of man. Interaction starts with life itself: it sustains, it is the world of child and parent, of youth and maturity as well. No emphasis was placed on the individual as if he were apart from society, because society was contained within every interaction. Interaction is, by definition, the social relation of at least two people.

Tautological? Perhaps. Nonetheless, the analysis conveniently resolved a host of problems. It provided a theory of the person; it explained the similarity of self and society; it made psychology social and, at the same time, suggested how society 'got into' the minds of men.

In the theory the person is a bridge: he embodies two sets of abstractions that had traditionally been labelled 'individual' and 'social'. As an individual he has acquired a character from the roles he has learned and appropriated; as a representative of his society (American, African, Burmese, Eskimo) he has developed roles from the repertoire made available by his social environment.

Interaction theory with its accompanying principles of social learning, role acquisition and role development supplies a social psychology that permits moving beyond elementary social behaviour and tiresome controversy concerning the priority of individual or group. Role theory in itself has a splendid neutrality. It may be stated objectively, from the standpoint of society. We speak then of role as a position to be filled, a job to be done, a function to be performed. It may also be stated subjectively – from the standpoint of the individual. We speak then of learning a role, or taking a role or performing one.

We see, too, why, in terms of role theory, the 'problem' of individuality and conformity, as it has been formulated in the past, becomes an essentially false problem. In order to function at all, all groups require roles to be performed; in fact, we may simply define the group in terms of individuals taking roles or performing functions. We cannot isolate the individual from his role taking; we can only state his options or choices, accepting or rejecting the alternative group life provides him. Generally speaking, we tend to overestimate his sphere of freedom. We may reject any number of specific roles, and this rejection is certainly an important freedom. But in doing so, we invariably take on others; that is, we can never wholly escape the definitions society constructs for us.* True nonconformity is, in this sense, nonexistent in the logic of role theory. Hermits, anchorites and monks represent extreme role restriction or role rejection but do not escape role definition. Society 'names' them. What is conventionally called nonconformity has – as the role theorist invariably points out – strong roots in small groups of all sorts, bohemians and beats, cults and clubs; that is, the nonconformist almost always attaches himself 'to fellow nonconformists with whom he conforms'.

By the same logic it is futile to engage in debate on the alleged conformity or nonconformity of whole groups, for whom, usually, degrees and direction of deviation from norm are such a strong part of role definition that we scarcely notice until roles are in the process of being redefined. Sex roles (men versus women) and age roles (the young versus the old) are strongly ascriptive – degrees of constriction and direction of deviance are built into them. Thus, the indivi-

* Hence, as Dahrendorf observed, 'The fact of society is vexatious'.

34

dualist male is conforming and so, too, are rebellious youth.*

Hence, to conform or not to conform is never the question in social life: conformity to what is the question that matters. The restrictions we usually term 'conformist' stem not from personal or psychological or biological sources but from social ones. 'Traditionalism', 'conventionality' and 'consistency' all represent types of role restriction; age, sex, and certain occupational categories present descriptions in these terms. So do marginal status groups and minorities whose ascribed roles often require or elicit a stereotyped conformity in some areas but relative freedom in others. The advantage of role theory is that it shifts our view of conformity as a trait and attaches it as a differential requirement of role performance or as a role response in specific situations.

Conformity is decidedly within us (we call it 'social learning'), but it is an acquired knowledge of role performances, some of which demand uniform and stereotyped behaviours and responses and some of which permit leeway. The role of a soldier, a judge or a bureaucrat requires strict and conventional performances; so likewise, a model or a débutante. The freedom of the free professions extends beyond their job ties to permissive behaviours that accompany any form of free enterprise. As students we are permitted a wider range of behaviours than we can expect as career-bound adults whether attending professional meetings or cocktail parties. Places elicit appropriate responses of sobriety (church), merriment (parties), silence (libraries) or talkativeness (theatre lobbies). There is, as we say, a time and a place for everything. There are other specific situations that elicit a 'conformity response' that can only be meaningfully related to the situation itself. Such uniformities appear in extreme situations, such as deprivation and disaster, in crowd behaviour, and in social psychology experiments. Their explanation remains obscure and controversial. A lively social psychology could hardly thrive on the ambiguities of such marginally social

* T. Parsons 'institutionalized deviance' – but in 'role logic', a contradiction in terms.

35

behaviour. Evidence of the shaping power of groups and organizations and institutions abounded, but as a social psychology, these revelations were elaborated as a psychology of role learning and a sociology of role structure. It is to this kind of analysis that we now turn.

PART II

Roles

4

Character and Society

'ONCE UPON A TIME', we might well begin, social life presented itself in stable and predictable forms. Roles belonged to the theatre, not to ordinary routine social existence where men knew their parts and therefore did not reflect upon taking them. The idea of character was uncomplicated, too, because it did not emphasize inner and outer man, private and public selves; it took time for discord, disconnection and conflict to be developed as 'characterization'. Thus, the characterology that has come to us from antiquity is as flat and unrevealing as the fable; it lacks inwardness and depth; it is all surface presentation.

All of these transformations by which, in time, character has been driven inward do not simply reflect changes in religiosity or idealism. Nor do they represent simply the history of an idea. They may instead be said to reflect the forms of social life itself. Character was once the social face of man, external and 'given'. It became, in time, inward, mysterious, and ineffable.

A look at these changes in literature may help us trace these transformations in character. The rounding out of character – in its literary form, the only record we have of past conceptions – largely describes the development of the novel. It is the literary home of character development – at first viewed mostly from outside (the great nineteenth-century 'social novels') and then inside (the modern psychological novel with its interior monologue and stream of consciousness).

Characterization was at first thoroughly embedded in social milieu. Formally, its psychology was limited (it thrived on 'ruling passions'); but had the social novel simply been the depiction of morals and manners we might today read them as guidebooks, hardly as entertainments. But they live on. We are accustomed to being told that their immortality comes from the artfulness of the writer or the skilful blending of character with time and place, and doubtless this is true. But how is it achieved? The developed character is either a caricature whose individual and social characteristics are so 'pure' we find them funny, or they prove to be mixed and complex types. The question we ask is: How was this complexity achieved long before psychologists invented introspection and discovered the inner self and long before it was decent or acceptable to portray these publicly?

We are not suggesting that men were not formerly thoughtful, reflective and inward-turning. They were almost required to be since displays of feeling and declarations of private conviction belong to a later period, closer to our own. Character, then, was developed externally, and it was usually shown through conflict, or disharmony, or multiplicity of roles. We may cite some examples:

1. While the novel is often called a vehicle of middle-class life, this is, at best, a half-truth. The novel is a fine sociological source because it provides for us now what it provided for the reader then – a panorama of society, a cross-section of types. The complex or difficult character is the one who does not or will not stay in place. He (or she) leaps and bounds across class barriers, moves up and down and around a social order we had assumed was closed and rigidly set. The hero may be as virtuous as David Copperfield making his way in the world or tough and roguish as a character from Balzac – but he moves. His varied experiences introduce him to ways of 'seeing and being'. They also confront him (and us) with a show of pure and impure types, harmonious and unharmonious men, those who grace and those who disgrace their assigned roles. Hence Thackeray's caustic observations *after* he has shown one of his characters (Sir Pitt Crawley) at

work, at leisure, and at home (and in conversation with tenants and workmen, women and relatives):

> Vanity Fair – Vanity Fair! Here was a man who could not spell and did not care to read – who had the habits and the cunning of a boor: whose aim in life was pettifogging: who never had a taste, or emotion, or enjoyment, but what was sordid and foul; and yet he had rank, and honours, and power, somehow: and was a dignitary of the land, and a pillar of the state. He was high sheriff, and rode in a golden coach. Great ministers and statesmen courted him; and in Vanity Fair he had a higher place than the most brilliant genius or spotless virtue.

2. The disharmony between role as it was supposed to be played (the noble character) and as it actually was leads directly to another major source of character complexity – multiple roles and hypocrisy. Contrary to our usual definition that this consists of the difference between what one says and what one does, hypocrisy shows up in action (not in thought) and is usually shown by portraying a character in his different, separate roles. The development of character in the Victorian novel so often depends on this kind of overt disharmony that hypocrisy is almost its hallmark. The 'secret vice' and the 'hidden life', the 'other side' of the upright man are all examples. They were unfolded dramatically, acted out in the daily life of the person. If a person represses his conflicts, we have neurosis; if he lives them out in different roles we have a mild form of dissociation. Our point here is only to emphasize the complete externalization of character. Conflict and complexity were there, but far from being 'buried within', they were shown and 'shown up'.

Consider Butler's representation of the character of T. Pontifex, parson. We are told little about the fellow's 'feeling' ('The habit of not admitting things to himself has become a confirmed one with him') except that

> He does not feel that he is in his element. The farmers look as if they were in their element. They are full-bodied, healthy and contented; but between him and them there is a great gulf fixed. A hard and drawn look begins to settle about the corners of his

mouth, so that even if he were not in a black coat and white tie a child might know him for a parson.

Are we shown a vocational interest test or a nondirective interview to get at his unhappiness in his work? Not at all. We are given instead a description of his daily habits:

> He has no taste for any of those field sports which were not considered unbecoming for a clergyman forty years ago. He does not ride, nor shoot, nor fish, nor course, nor play cricket. Study, to do him justice, he had never really liked. . . .
> True he writes his own sermons but even his wife considers that his *forte* lies rather in the example of his life (which is one long act of self-devotion) than in his utterances from the pulpit.

What does he do every day? 'After breakfast he retires to his study; he cuts little bits out of the Bible and gums them with exquisite neatness by the side of other little bits; this he calls making a Harmony of the Old and New Testaments.' And: 'He heard his children their lessons, and the daily oft-repeated screams that issue from the study during the lesson hours tell their own horrible story over the house' (Butler). Now if you are tempted from the above description to venture your own psychodiagnosis, you are but a child of your own time. That is another matter. Here we only wish to show how the author develops his character without any reference whatsoever to psychic states or to feelings but simply to behaviours in the course of a typical day. His 'role enactments' are quite sufficient to give a complex picture of 'character'.

3. Finally, we come upon the modern character. His roles are no more complex, nor are his relationships, nor his habits; but each of these is likely to be worked and reworked from every direction, inside and out, and, of course, from the standpoint of others as well as from the character and the author. The representation has 'grown bigger' and we can tell why with a small fragment from Joyce's *Ulysses*:

> He crossed to the bright side, avoiding the loose cellar-flap of number seventy-five. The sun was nearing the steeple of George's church. Be a warm day I fancy. Specially in these black clothes

feel it more. Black conducts, reflects (refracts is it?) the heat. But I couldn't go in that light suit. Make a picnic of it. His eyelids sank quietly often as he walked in happy warmth. Boland's breadvan delivering with trays our daily but she prefers yesterday's loaves turnovers crisp crowns hot. Makes you feel young. Somewhere in the east: early morning: set off at dawn, travel round in front of the sun, steal a day's march on him. Keep it up for ever never grow a day older technically. Walk along a strange, strange land, come to a city gate, sentry there, old ranker too, old Tweedy's big moustaches leaning on a long kind of a spear. Wander through awned streets. Turbaned faces going by. Dark caves of carpet shops, big man. Turko the terrible, seated crosslegged smoking a coiled pipe. Cries of sellers in the streets. Drink water scented with fennel, sherbet. Wander along all day. Might meet a robber or two. Well, meet him. Getting on to sundown. The shadows of the mosques along the pillars: priests with a scroll rolled up. A shiver of the trees, signal, the evening wind. I pass on. Fading gold sky. A mother watches from her doorway. She calls her children home in their dark language. High wall: beyond strings twanged. Night sky moon, violet, colour of Molly's new garters. Strings. Listen. A girl playing one of these instruments what do you call them: dulcimers. I pass.

That's Bloom, of course, 'simply' strolling down the street: his movement and his movements of thought inform us of the casual compunctions of his character; but 'character' stands for much more. It bears the weight of culture-history brought to life by his free associations: day and night, youth and age, woman and man, East and West appear and disappear. The 'story' is an account of one full day, and we can see why it takes so long to tell: nothing is to be excluded, the boundaries of character constantly shift, everything 'moves', in interplay.

Character complexity can be achieved through role analysis working from the outside or through elaborations within that incorporate the external world. Either way the boundaries between the individual and the social give way; new definitions of their interrelations are sought, new meanings of character emerge.

Social Change and Character

The social changes that accompanied the changed 'psychology of man' – his modernization – are usually summarized in the term 'individualization': economically, a man became a separate earner or worker or producer; politically, an independent citizen; legally, a free and individual person. All of these aspects indicated his emancipation from old legal or kinship or communal ties and traditions. At the same time, such a division of person into various roles – economic, political, legal – was the preparatory ground for the general distinction between private and public, inner and outer, what a man 'is' and what he 'does', and all other terms we use or have used to describe the discontinuities between man in his strictly individual and man in his social aspect. 'Individual psychology' arose, too, taking for granted the social separation of man and, in its own way, endorsing his eternal egoism (as the 'nature of man'). Yet psychology was but another aspect of the division of labour that used men's bodies and minds 'to their most efficient purpose'. 'Consciousness' became a problem too, as did 'mind'.

How is it, we ask, once mind ceased to be an abstraction, that we came to 'know' the mind only in terms of what it does, or can do: it can add and subtract numbers, form or imagine ideas, put words together or unscramble them; it can remember and it can forget; it has multiple coordinate 'functions' – eye to hand, ear to voice, nose to taste, and so on. Thus mind becomes a holding company of capacities or functions or factors, each viewed in increasingly specialized form. Once separated from the man, the loquacity of the lawyer, the verbiage of the writer, the colour imagery of the artist are no different from the hand of the skilled machinist or the sculptor. When we no longer think of lawyer, writer, artist, machinist but his special aspect – his verbal facility, his colour imagery, his manual dexterity – then we are thinking 'psychologically', and we are altogether modern.

Thus, sociologists have linked these definitions and forms of 'consciousness' to the evolving structure of society itself –

specifically, in the past, to the division of labour, new technologies, and an industrial order that gradually elaborated new social relations and social roles. We have been generously provided with a nomenclature to describe this massive social change from old to new societies (status to contract, *gemeinschaft* to *gesellschaft*) and the 'character' and 'consciousness' that also changed. The character of man became a special part of him as he became specialized: it moved inward; it became elaborately structured.

In recent time this has come full circle: 'character', for example, appears to have lost its narrow psychological significance and has increasingly been endowed social content and meaning. New theories of 'social character' were invented to stand alongside it, drastically modifying the freedom with which individual character might be conceived to express itself and often obscuring the differences between the two. 'Growing up' we now call, simply, socialization. The new extroversion of the character principle has largely been accomplished by the critical resetting of its terms and by new differentiations and definitions of self.

Old Self, New Selves*

In the past, all self theories sought to locate and explain an unchanging identity of person, inner and invisible, that surpassed growth and maturity, withstood time and circumstance and endured despite manifest external transformations. Its inward emphasis implied an abstract self for whose understanding historic and social circumstance may be regarded as totally irrelevant. But attempts to grasp an inner identity that, unlike the physical person, does not change were first made problematic by the great modern psychologists. Their psychologies of self created a world of great subjective complexity: for James, the self was many selves; and Freudian psychoanalytic theory, which greatly contributed to shatter-

* This section is adapted from my earlier article, 'The Problem of Personality in Sociological Theory', in Wepman and Heine (1963), pp. 388–93.

ing traditional conceptions of the self, above all dramatized the complex interplay between its inner and outer expression. From the sociological standpoint, the interesting aspect of all inward-turning descriptions of self, person, or personality is that they all tend to obscure rather than reveal the ordinary, everyday processes by which we identify others and are identified by them: name and gesture, place and role. Moreover, all alike lay claim to the doubtful proposition that inner life is more durable and more determining than outward circumstance in describing and explaining the conduct of men.

The 'personality factor', as it has come to be called, sets clear limitations. To represent personality as an independent force in life not only implies ignoring all those external conditions that may, in fact, limit and shape it, but also (so it has been argued) forces us into paths of fruitless speculation concerning the nature of self that changes and yet always remains the same. Most doctrines of self, of character or of personality that described or sought to describe something independent and immutable within the person have stumbled over the problem of change. If the self changes, if there is no inner nucleus or ego that remains constant, what meaning can we attach to old theories of the self? Bergsonian philosophy called the subjective self in its endless flux the only sure reality. Freudian theory viewed the self as an uneasy and precarious balance of conflicting forces; but behaviourism simply denied its existence and set both psychology and social psychology to the task of defining the empirical person.

The specific sociological contribution to the redefinition of self and personality is called 'social behaviourism'. Identified with George Herbert Mead, who approached, as he said, experience 'from the standpoint of society' instead of the psychological standpoint of individual experience, is the theory that mind, consciousness and self are to be regarded as products of the social process of communication and the shared experience that comes from taking the role of others. In theory and in practice it has meant that we turn our attention outward, that we forgo discussion of what man is and look instead at what he does.

Since the theory rests strongly on the principle of internalization, it is perhaps an error to over-emphasize contrasts between inner and outer, covert and overt, for these were precisely the old terms, as troublesome as they were irrelevant. The fact is that both aspects obtained and were retained in everything we call social. But we no longer look within the person for our generalizing propositions; we look instead to social situations and social behaviours, and we eschew relating (consistencies of) behaviour to the presumed psychic structure of the person at all. 'Social behaviourism' is, in this sense and this alone, 'behaviouristic'. Meaning is revealed in action; minds develop through social interaction.

Not only the confused state of personality theory itself but its assumptions led to this reformulation of old problems. Behind all character and personality theory is the assumption that, in given social situations, it is the propensities one brings to the situation that count, not the specific demands of the situation or the definition of roles within it. Hence, if there may be said to be a uniquely sociological approach to personality, it is to be found in emphasis on personality as process and on a method based on the analysis of situations in terms of action and reaction among the participants. Character type or personal inclination, from the sociological viewpoint, are seen as irrelevant to understanding behaviour since what the actors bring to a given social situation matters less than the types of interaction that become established between them. Role analysis is, then, an alternative to character or personality analysis.

Within the field of psychology itself considerable support came to be mustered for role analysis. Character and personality theories have been more conspicuous than invigorating in the psychologist's approach to social psychology. The search for inner unity, pattern or coherence issued in a great play of competing typologies; for the rest, personality theory was bogged down by the complex problems of trait analysis and trait measurement. It was not only role theory that favoured 'situational' analysis; that individual behaviour may be better defined in terms of a 'field' of forces (as in Lewinian theory) implied another forsaking of traditional trait psychology and old characterology. Both converged in the theory and practice of small group research.

Strictly speaking, role theory is not antithetical to traditional character and personality theory, but in contrast to these it tends: (1) to emphasize the ongoing social process, the act, or the social situation, whereas most character and personality theories emphasize the impress of the individual self upon the act; and (2) to interpret social situations in terms of interaction with an analytically refined S-R theory as the point of departure. The actions and reactions set up between two or more people are significant, and reciprocity becomes the key point of analysis.

Role Theory and Character Theory

Role theory, from G. H. Mead onward, stands, then, in contrast to the relatively static interpretations of character and personality in that it stresses the shifting, mutually adaptive, transactional aspects of human relationships. The self is not viewed as a relatively rigid or structured unity but as a congeries of roles, capable of extension, flexible and adaptive. Where character and personality theory lends itself to interpretations in depth, role theory is oriented to notions of extension and differentiation of experience. We learn by taking the role of the other, and the self is an image we learn only through others – it is 'reflected appraisal'. Thus, too, the self is enriched not through inner cultivation or virtuosity but by its capacity to reach out, to participate broadly, to be gregarious.

Needless to say, role theory has not wholly dispensed with the idea of character and personality; instead character has been redefined in its external, active, dramatic sense. Shorn of the ideas of inwardness and autonomy, it is often equated with role performance. Roles may be consistent or discrepant (depending on the situation), harmonious or conflicting. In any case, to understand them, we need not explore the person as such but rather the various social contexts or levels on which he is functioning. While such theories may distinguish between actor as performer and actor as character, it is a distinction that is all but meaningless. Our character is our performance, and vice versa. Role theory is carried neatly and logically to these conclusions by Goffman in his *The Presentation of Self in Everyday Life* (1969).

Erving Goffman's contemporary extension of role-playing is bereft of the philosophical concerns of G. H. Mead and consists of a dramatic projection of social process as 'theatrical performance'. Goffman is a sociologist by training: there is much of G. H. Mead in his construction, but other aspects of his work appear as an application of Georg Simmel's 'sociability' principle to all of social life. Simmel (1858–1914) remains the most engaging of the German sociologists often referred to as the school of 'formal sociology'. In the search for a proper definition of the new field called sociology, he, among others, hit upon the conception of 'social forms'. Much of the content of the field was clearly shared with the old established social sciences: what was new and distinctive, so it was argued, was the analysis of types of interaction or social forms that appeared and reappeared in different historical and cultural contexts – hence the name pure or formal sociology. In focusing upon forms of interaction and types of social process, Simmel fathered a set of interests and concerns quite familiar to contemporary social psychologists. His analysis of dyads and triads and the influence of size (or number of members) on group process reappeared, in experimental form, in the small group research of the 1950s. His 'pure form' of social relation called 'sociability' also has its present-day counterpart in Goffman's work. Simmel called sociability a play-form; he remarked its democratic, give-and-take character – it was, he said, essentially a form of interaction among equals. Among its subtypes he included 'social games', an analysis of 'coquetry' and 'conversation' (Simmel, 1950, Chapter 3).

Thus, play and game and theatrical analogy appear

repeatedly in the 'sociological' social psychologists. We 'take parts', 'play games', 'interact'. The focus is not so much on the actor, however, as on the action. In moving from actor to actors, and act to action, role theory does not deny the notions of autonomy and wilfulness (voluntarism) in the social process, but in a none too subtle way these are denigrated, as prime movers, and put aside. The crucial instance here is the approach to the problem of leadership. This problem is a topic that Goffman avoids completely in favour of 'team analysis' (scanting heroes and captains alike). He speaks first of all of 'lonely' performances, which he calls 'one-man teams' – the person has no colleagues 'to inform his decisions'. 'Larger teams' require collusion and cooperation, and Goffman gives us many examples from medical to concert performances, but as yet no principle of dominance is introduced. Finally, we learn that 'when one examines a team-performance, one often finds that someone is given the right to direct and control the progress of the dramatic action' (p. 84). This includes directors of weddings, funerals, parties and sports events (the umpire): we are on the sidelines of performances but not yet 'in them'. Presently, he does introduce 'the star, lead, or centre of attention', and we learn that '. . . those who help present a team-performance differ in the degree of dramatic dominance given each of them and . . . one team-routine differs from another in the extent to which differentials in dominance are given its members' (p. 88). These differences between 'dramatic' and 'directive' dominance may be understood somewhat better if we compare them with the role differentiations we find in small group research. There, too, leadership is viewed neither as power nor as moving personal force nor as a personal trait. There, too, it becomes a group function – now 'emotional' or 'instrumental' – but each is defined in terms of the criteria by which it is measured. Where we have multiple determinism (stated as reciprocity or interaction) we cannot at the same time emphasize the unique and the singular. The 'group process' or the 'team performance' is a spectacle. The play's the thing.

In the interest in scene, situation and presentation, we can certainly observe some parallel limitations. Thus the analytic refinements of Goffman's work may occasion the protest that too great a halo of ceremony, etiquette and decorum is cast over all social relationships, that in so doing we are given depictions of social roles that are too rigid. Moreover, its shallowness and lack of depth, particularly in contrast to stratified theories of the self, have often been criticized. There are other difficulties, too, and we may touch upon them here because they explain a basic discomfiture of the sociologist *vis-à-vis* his 'own' social psychology.

Criticism of Dramaturgical Theory

Distinctively sociological social psychologies have always occupied a rather special and limited framework within the field of sociology itself. Characteristically 'formal' and 'abstract' (like the general forms of the old 'formal sociologists'), their psychology derives not from syphoning social experience through the individual psyche (as faculty, drive, motive, or conditioned response) but of tracing the common meanings of pattern or form in human interaction or social experience through the gamut of its expressions – from the most personal to the most abstract, from the covert to the overt, latent to manifest, immediate to secondary or even tertiary effects. It generates its psychology in a roundabout way and is often, on the surface, anti-psychological, denying priority to the unique individual and disparaging the bondage of traditional psychology to biology.

Their psychology moved beyond these perspectives, once again underwriting the 'autonomy of the social', by substituting social for biological psychology. With the emergence of the institutional order as a 'third force' (separate and irreducible as biology), the content of the 'psychological' changes too. The individual becomes the carrier of (common) meaning and the actor of (common) roles and so loses his centrality and uniqueness. At the same time, clear lines between psychic and social are blurred.

51

We shall be first concerned with centrality. It is instructive for the student to re-examine here the way in which personal and social behaviour is analytically approached without the benefit and blessing of character and personality, drive and impulse, wish and motive. Here the rediscovery of the familiar is based upon the interpretation of surface behaviours in terms of immediate confrontation and interaction where set and stage and script – socially instituted and prescribed – appear as given. The drama of social life no longer unfolds through the eyes of the actor but comes to life through analysis of whole scene and prop and setting. Thus our definition of character springs not from the actor himself but from all those external characteristics that define and complete his role, not least of all, the actions of others. As in the tale of the prince and the pauper (and in countless cases of highly successful impersonations in real life), we are what we appear to be.

Of course, were this an adequate account of social life, rather than certain aspects of it, the art of impression management could become quite scientific, and a host of moral problems would simply vanish. Our conceptions of sincerity as well as hypocrisy would disappear and the over- or under-playing of roles would become simply stylistic nuances. But real social differences, as well as personal ones, tend to disappear in this social psychology, both alike absorbed as 'social process'.

We next turn to uniqueness. In relation to traditional views of personality, the question inevitably arises of just what is left if we do try to separate person from role and prop, scene and setting. For analytic purposes, the person is treated as if he had no history; biography gives way to interaction process. But often, too, this isolation of the person from his personal history is paralleled by his removal from particular institutional and organizational settings, and we are left with an impoverished scheme of motivation – often reduced to the terms 'the show must go on' or 'keeping the game going'.

Hence to sociologists, too, this dramaturgical theory may present a disturbing amorphousness. The institutional orders are not quite reducible to the play of various social psychological forms, no matter by what name they are called – patterns, types of interaction, rules of the game. This troublesome fact will be revealed at once in the favoured metaphors of the play, the game, and the team, for they disguise precisely what the sociologist often chooses as his revealed truth: we may cherish the belief in our own power without really having power; we may dream of the capacity to manage and manipulate but not have that capacity. Only small portions of social life are truly analogous to games and play. Our exits and entrances are neither so voluntary nor so capricious as the analogy suggests. And if it is true that the bindingness of rules remains the valid point of analogy, its 'as if' premises (as if we entered social life by mutual agreement, as if we joined the team) tend to obscure problems of structure and organization, leadership and domination, power and prestige – all of which seemingly wither away in the directness and intimacy of interaction. Having removed the coercive weight of institution and organization, order and ritual are referred not to their real source (living men who live out the aims of the organizations in which they participate) but to process as such ('the game must go on'). The result is emphasis on ongoingness, and also on artifice and masquerade, the superficially motivated ritualism of social life.

Nonetheless, vestiges of old individualism remain, even with the following provisions:

1. Retention of wilful and voluntary factors may be seen in the notion of 'playing it right'; against this is invoked the arbitrariness of rules (of game, of team, of society).

2. Retention of individual mastery appears in the notion of manipulating and managing scenes and presentations; against this are arrayed set and props and relations to other actors that limit its exercise.

3. Retention of the idea of spontaneity is seen via ongoingness of act and interaction; against this, of course, are the formal rules of the game that preclude an excess of surprise, caprice, and chance.

Concerning theatre and life we might well ask what is the

53

attractiveness of this old analogy and what is its merit. Respect for the genius of Shakespeare? An eye for the vanity and falsity of social life? A profound pessimism toward the aims and purposes of men who are 'mere players'? We have touched upon some of the disadvantages of seeing life as theatre: it gives us a wholly inadequate view of social structure while it busily elaborates social process. But it may be instructive to recall that if social life is not so much theatre, nonetheless theatre is part of social life. As a social institution, we may glimpse in it the why and wherefore of the analogy.

Suppose, then, we insist upon the analogy 'all the world's a stage and all the men and women merely players'. Suppose we go further and compare in detail the actor and the person, turning momentarily to the position of the professional actor. In the past, he stood outside the established estates, and his occupational life mirrored the instability of his real life. Belonging nowhere, he wandered. Unattached to a fixed role (in the eyes of others), he tried many. The moral disapprobation associated with the profession has long endured: distrust of the free and the footloose, suspicion of the actor's lack or loss of attachment to place and tradition, his presumptive moral lapse followed accordingly. Just as surely as an ordinary stable occupation precluded the role taking of the actor, so diverse role taking disabled one for ordinary occupations. We might say, then, that it has taken a very long time to distinguish the person of the actor from his occupation. *A man of many roles and many parts has no stable and reliable character.*

Preliminarily, we might agree that the mobility of modern life itself suggests the analogy. In making role our central social concept, we are in effect saying that we have all become strolling actors in a society in which no one feels quite at home. We set forth the comparison as shown in the table on p. 55.

On the surface, the analogy seems apt. Our central column summarizes things very nicely. It traces the relationship between objective social fact and subjective experience. A

54

man moving to a new post may incur approval from colleagues for 'moving up', but disapproval from close kin or
friends for 'moving away'. He is not necessarily sure what is
'right'. Moving to a new place creates new role tests for him.
Will he be accepted? Will he fit in? Will he have to 'toe the
line' or can he be his 'old self'? He may have to take on a
'new identity', dressing somewhat differently, acquiring the
right kind of house in the right kind of neighbourhood and
associating with the right kind of friends in clubs and
churches and organizations. If he does not make such changes
easily, he does not 'fit', and he is almost certain to feel
uneasy and conflicted.

ACTOR	ROLE	PERSON
versatility	mobility – instability many roles – many parts unreliable character – unstable character structure	fragmentation
		identity crisis
masks or faces?		(Who am I?)

Such role analysis (Whyte made it quite familiar in his
Organization Man) goes far to explain common experiences
and common conflicts, and it does so without reference to
personality. Typically, there is no conflict, for as Whyte also
pointed out, the person is realistic, he conforms, he gets on
with the show. It may be, then, that we need only a personality theory to explain conflict and maladaptation.

There is reason, however, to suspect that we do not yet
have the whole 'personality story', and we shall show why by
moving to the other side of our scheme above – the side of
the actor. There is, in the literature of the theatre, a notable
'paradox of acting' that has been debated time and time
again: Does the actor 'live' his parts or just 'imitate' them?
Does he have a personality that invigorates his role-playing,
or is he just a genius of impersonation? And what is meant
by a 'poor actor'? How is it (if his personality counts so

little) that a man can follow all the rules, do everything correctly and yet be 'just a ham actor'? Obviously, so the argument runs, there is more to acting than role, more than just imitation. There are faces behind the masks (Archer, 1888).

The face-behind-the-mask argument is exactly like the social-psychological argument of personality versus role. We cite it because role theory is often used to explain away the personal by turning to the theatrical. If we turn to the theatre, however, we confront the same dilemma that we come upon in social life: good and bad performances cannot altogether be explained by setting, props, technical effects and supporting cast. In theatre, as in life, we find no easy solution to the problem of personality.

Is role everything? Sometimes it is. Complete absorption in role is usually interpreted as (a) conventionality (the 'lady', the 'bureaucrat', the 'judge'), or as (b) sincerity or consistency (the 'pure' artist, the 'true' believer); and, conversely, role distance is customarily viewed as prerequisite for (a) playing roles (an actor or actress), or (b) conscious deceit, manipulation or fraud (the con man). Traditionally, upper-class life and middle-class modes, with insistence on the domain of privacy, worked on the assumption that roles were roles and duties were duties, but left some margin through withdrawal in time (leisure) and space (privacy). Character and personality were hardly problems. Under conditions of modern life, we seldom know the person in all his roles; hence, we become distrustful of his many-sidedness, and we seek desperately for an organizing principle (personality theory) that might give some kind of stability to myriad pictures of the role-taking person. Sometimes this principle has been sought as 'core' or 'centre', sometimes as 'lifestyle', sometimes as a characteristic pattern set firm through 'primary socialization'. To these matters we shall return later.

We come last to deception. An interesting aspect of Goffman's presentation is that it is often viewed as cynical and as itself playful. In focusing on the surface forms and rituals of social life, it encourages our disbelief in surface meaning, in sincerity or trust, and the sociologist seems to be telling us that he is going to let us in on the secrets of social life. He emphasizes forms of gamesmanship and deception, of playing around with roles, not just playing them. In going along with him, we too can easily lose sight of the fact that this is but one view of some aspects of life. We might also agree that the conditions of modern life make such experiences increasingly common: our relationships with others are tangential and one-sided; our knowledge of facts and situations is often inadequate. Moreover, it is true that because of these lacks, we have become increasingly distrustful of others; we learn to play it safe, keep our distance, reserve our judgement, and pretend. Nonetheless, if playing games were the whole story, we should lack all criteria for distinguishing fraud, pretension, and the confidence game. The con man, as a matter of fact, becomes more than an interesting case (Goffman has subjected him to careful analysis elsewhere); he is an important paradigm because 'while the performance offered by impostors and liars is quite flagrantly false and differs in this respect from ordinary performances, both are similar in the care their performers must exert in order to maintain the impression that is fostered' (p. 57–8). Many objections might be raised to this assertion: we might observe, for example, that 'ordinary' performers do not scrutinize their performances in this way at all – the performances are natural or ingrained; or we might suggest that the least important aspect of true and false performances is what they share merely as performances. We may have somewhat better luck observing the relevance of the con man by following Thomas Mann's portrayal in *Confessions of Felix Krull*.

We may again remark the association with mobility: here the literary case history is built upon two social facts – the absence of fixed social place and the experienced loss of it. Young Krull is sharply uprooted: he is *déclassé*. Gradually he learns the uses of personal charm (once part of the charmed existence of his early childhood) and its influence in making his own way in a hard world. A critical experience, moreover, while he serves as a waiter in a Parisian hotel is his sudden imaginative insight into the fortuitous aspects of social roles. How easy to change positions, he observes, while he waits on others! And, in changing position, how automatically one assumes a new identity! He acquires, in fact, the very insight of the sociologist:

My basic attitude toward the world and society can only be called inconsistent. For all my eagerness to be on affectionate terms with them, I was frequently aware of a considered coolness, a tendency to critical reflection, which astonished me. There was, for example, an idea that occasionally preoccupied me when for a few leisure moments I stood in the lobby or dining hall, clasping a napkin behind my back and watching the hotel guests being waited and fawned upon by blue-liveried minions. It was the idea of *interchangeability*. With a change of clothes and make-up, the servitors might often just as well have been the masters, and many of those who lounged in the deep wicker chairs, smoking their cigarettes, might have played the waiter. It was pure accident that the reverse was the fact, an accident of wealth; for an aristocracy of money is an accidental and interchangeable aristocracy.

As can be seen, the realization makes for cool appraisal, for role analysis, and for a playful attitude toward life. The real question is, if this is social truth, what makes us stay in our places? And if taking on roles is just a 'cognitive' problem, what is the place of moral scruple?

The fact is that the apparent cynicism of this kind of analysis comes from our being asked to see the similarity, not the difference, between the con game and the game of social life. It seems that just as the power of the institutional order is slighted, so too are its moral accompaniments. If we are rooted in social position, we are ordinarily also instructed in its moral rules and requirements. We are not free to pick and choose the rules. Our learning of roles (called 'socialization') may be weak or strong or confused: we recognize these differences, by the way, as differences in personal history and personality.

The critical status of person, and the so-called problem of personality, have evolved from the same specialization that has marked the disappearance of our common world. The person is no longer 'of a piece'. Those things that in the past organized our experience of the person – biography, the character(ization) of a novel, the theatre – have also changed. Sometimes they have mirrored, sometimes heralded new interpretations. The theatre of the absurd, for example, proceeds in exactly opposite fashion to conventional dramaturgy. It shows us 'essential humanity' by denuding the stage, not outfitting it. With character, so too with social structure, both go. We are left with the existential question of authenticity at every level.

In sum, the shifting boundaries of the person (our uncertainty about his character) apparently derive from the complex roles the person plays, and his mobility in and between them. We may translate the meaning of shifting boundaries to everyday experiences: our relationships with others are often fleeting, or specialized (for work, play, domesticity), but it is seldom that we see people 'in the round', know their many sides or all their roles. Puzzlement about the meaning of relationship is therefore painfully common: if we try to move beyond the specialized relation defined as work obligation or play companionship, membership association or kinship duty, our moves are tentative and uncertain. They may be out of line; they may be encouraged; they may be rebuffed – it is the absence of knowingness or certainty that is important. Fragmentation into roles seems to lead either to narrow role adherence, a kind of over-conformity, or to those caprices we recognize as 'testing behaviours'. The latter consist of trying (but not trying too hard), of investing (but not too much), or caring (but not over-caring). Such 'playful' attitudes we call role distance or role detachment.

Only when our experience replicates that of the strolling actor or the con man do we get the kind of role detachment that submerges personality in role taking. Only, at the other extreme, does complete and conventionalized role absorption achieve the same effect. In both cases, the coincidence of role and personality seems to make the concept of personality superfluous. We shall show the social ground between the two by reviewing how socialization theory works out the problems of person, role and personality. It is in this area that the debate has come to be centred.

5

Socialization

THE original analogy to play and games was not intended as a model for all of society but as a paradigm of social learning. For Mead, it is first of all a theory of socialization and a description of the way in which the self becomes like others, yet, in the critical capacity to judge and test and choose, retains its 'selfhood'. That critical capacity is only learned through try-outs: role learning comes through role taking, and so we build from immediate 'significant others' to the 'generalized other' (the community) – linguistic terms, passing from mere imitation to 'significant gesture', sign, and symbol where common meaning emerges because the same response is aroused in self and other.

The derivation of the self, or personality, through social process, through cooperative activity, and through identical reactions of the self and others has proved a useful description. It tells us how and from whom we learn our 'parts', and therefore how we come eventually to 'take our place' in society. In contrast to other theories of personality, this description emphasizes the social source of personality without being doctrinaire about its details. It involves no strict endorsement of developmental phases, sequences or stages. Mythic processes are absent – no Oedipus, no totemic horde, no authoritarian drama. The process described is ordinary social interchange; the casual not the melodramatic aspects of growing up are emphasized; and it is plainly democratic in its emphasis on give and take, learning and sharing, play and games. Its unique contribution was its philosophical analysis of the act from which were derived the theory of language, communication, and the 'meaning of meaning'. These last aspects have never figured importantly in socialization theory. The role concept and role learning have.

The last two concepts have come to be a supporting pillar of much contemporary social psychology. They mediate the social process (social role learning) and describe its internalization. Role theory can accommodate either a strong behavioural approach, emphasizing that what we are is what we have learned; or it can be joined with a more elaborate psychodynamics to enlarge the details of role learning and internalization. The conjunction of role and psychoanalytic doctrine has been made effective through the work of the psychiatrist, Harry Stack Sullivan. In sociology, these views were similarly forwarded by Hans Gerth and G. Wright Mills (1954) and were made systematic by Talcott Parsons (Parsons *et al.*, 1956). Their present diffusion has resulted in diffuseness. The assimilation of role and personality theory has sometimes been pressed so far that the distinction between the two is all but lost. Theories emphasizing role competence and role choice often present a confusing blend. Such zealous attempts to establish harmony 'between the spheres' are not uncommon these days, but we shall cite only one example of it and pass on. In *Role Development and Interpersonal Competence*, an experimental study of role performance in a small group, Moment and Zaleznik (1963) move role and personality concepts to and fro so freely that the line between the two is entirely lost. We follow their path and find that in early development, role taking is set down as a 'predisposition'. Predisposition is a personality concept not a role concept, but this departure from role theory is presently corrected by converting predisposition to eventual role specialization. Role specialization, in turn, can be recognized in a small group experiment as a role type. Another name for a role type is style of interpersonal behaviour (style, however, is a personality idea); hence, we are led back into quite pure personality interpretations, and an array of personality tests, to interpret role performance in a group. What, then, is the difference between role and personality?

Let us start at the beginning with the question of role choice. As a theory of socialization, the proponents of role analysis have seldom been accused of emphasizing choice. The interaction process – from beginning to end, from mother and child to conversation of the aged – is 'open-ended'; it is changeful; it is ongoing. The relationship within which that process is going on is probably not chosen. These are the relationships, quite ordinary everyday ones, that embody what the sociologist otherwise calls the routine constraints of social life. They are our social bonds; they root us in family, in class, in milieu, in region.

We need not be so formal about the institutional 'ties that bind'. We can get at the matter by putting a few direct questions. Suppose we ask: Do I choose to be born? Do I choose my parents? my birthplace? where I go to school? From the very beginning, the principle of role learning implies little about choice. Our introduction to society is through role models presented to us, and these we cannot pick and choose. But when and where can one pick and choose? Clearly a child cannot. Technically, a child can run away from home (and become a ward of the state); or he can refuse to go to school (thereby becoming a potential candidate for a special school or a detention home). Suppose, further, we follow the old plaint or the child's dream, 'When I grow up, I'll do just what I want.' We hesitate to enumerate the disenchantments that may await him between the tender ages of eighteen and twenty-one, for the young are the first to inform us, after all, of the irony of their choices. Going to school or being drafted in the army, staying single and lonely or marrying and feeling constrained, choosing a career and becoming career-bound or simply drifting – obviously the world has failed in its options for youth! Does age fare better? Not noticeably, for the old are getting younger and younger. They may retire early, bored and disengaged, or they may be 'hangers on', stubborn old men; they may be independent and lonely, or they may be dependent and a burden to others. And so it goes.

We do, of course, have some choices (a career choice is always a favourite example), and some people who are favourably situated have many choices; but generally role analysis has led to no such emphasis. To the contrary: while not using the term role conscription, a systematic sociology formulates the question as one of institutional role requirements – there are social functions that have to be performed, duties that have to be fulfilled, work that has to be done – and of personal role taking, that is the enactments of persons who fill available or necessary positions. Role becomes the mediating concept of social psychology in the same way. The difference is that social psychologists make the idea of role more active and lively, and they almost always focus on role learning and role taking (the person) rather than on institutional requirements or the social allocation of roles. The last may seem particularly objectionable because it sounds as if there were a Central Planning Board administering social life. The personal act of role learning and role taking fits with jobs and tasks that have to be done through ongoing organizations.

There is another important source of regularity and co-ordination, and it, too, can be stated either from the side of role taking or role allocation. One reason why we 'stay in our places' is that the roles we take tend to be interconnected or reinforced by different institutions. These, again, are predictable regularities or probabilities that we recognize as role congruity. We arrive at them through the systematic collection of data that we correlate and cross-correlate. Suppose we take the conspicuous example of occupational role; from occupational role we may trace correlates of:

	INSTITUTION
a) income	economic
b) status	kinship
c) church affiliation	religious
d) political affiliation	political
e) club membership	interest or pressure group

The occupational role of worker, farmer or executive tends to carry with it a probable income, a typical social status, a likely religious affiliation (Catholic or Protestant), a political preference (Democrat or Republican). Usually, of course, we have to qualify our statement by referring to variables such as milieu; for example, big city workers are more often Catholic than Protestant, or Southern farmers are traditionally Democratic rather than Republican. The point is that we do find regular differences that lend themselves to interpretations of order and structure. Whether we proceed to emphasize the order as hierarchical (class, status, or power pyramids) or coordinate (structure or system) is another matter.

Such a description is quite remote from the questions we ordinarily raise about personality: first, because it is all surface data, and we tend to believe that personality is deep within us; and second, because we so live our roles that we cannot imagine there is anything obscure about them. But roles are not simple, and role congruity does not imply that personality simply disappears. Even those who maintain that personality is the sum of all our roles and how we manage them are far from suggesting that matters are thereby simplified.

The difficulty is of a different order. Role is an objective idea – a duty one takes on, a function one fills. Even if we state it from the standpoint of the acting person, it retains the quality of not-me; and even if we demonstrate it as an essential function one joyously takes on, it is still something taken on. These are the objections that are traditionally raised by personality theorists. They believe there is an 'inside story' – hence their pronounced aversion to an emphasis on role definition or role requirement. To demonstrate that inside story they usually go beyond notions of stylistic variation in role performance or the range of choice and option that society so providentially allows. They turn to the distinctiveness or autonomy of the person as they evolve through his life history. The question then becomes: How relevant is the life history and how lasting is its relevance to the way we enact our roles? Are there typical sequences or stages on the way to becoming a person? Are they generalizable over time and from place to place? As we shall see, the cumulative effect of socialization studies has not brought personality to the foreground but made it relative to time and place and circumstance. The idea of uniqueness, of the development of person in response to environmental conditions, has almost disappeared; the idea that the 'child is father to the man' endures as a metaphor because it tells us something about patterns of childhood, not the certain distinctiveness of *this* child or *this* man.

Types of self or person are reared, trained, bred, inculcated: there is no theory of person without a corresponding set of propositions describing how he came to be what he is. Beyond these propositions, however, rather different emphasis is placed depending on whether we focus on the functional or strictly historical aspects of 'becoming a person'. There is every indication that, aided and abetted by social changes that made sociological doctrines increasingly relevant, role theories of person and of socialization have come to supplant old ideas. Ongoingness, which implies that the present situation or function may have little to do with one's past, is reflected in the fact that the further we move from the circumstances of our childhood (from country to city, from city to suburb, from scarcity to abundance), the less relevance they have. Just as a conditioning history can be compressed into an experimental series that forces reinspection of the weight of long cumulative history, so our experiences after childhood have forced a reassessment of habits presumably set down permanently in early childhood. Social changes typically require adaptations we hardly recognize until long after they have occurred. It is clear that little in the early training or experience of a Southern black youth quite prepares him for his likely future role in the civil rights movement. Rigorous training for independence, so often presumed to be part of our general achievement orientation, does not appear very helpful to the future organization man. Thus our present attitudes toward the relevance of personal history are likely to be provisional. That revolution in attitude towards the world of childhood, ushered in by Freud, appears destined to revolve again.

Historically, there have been periods when children were regarded as miniature adults; still later, as creatures to be tamed and domesticated; and later again, as tough-tender plants to be grown and cared for and cultivated.* While role theories, as customarily presented, emphasize the incorporation of the social by the growing child, G. H. Mead had originally observed the way in which role theory obliges us to 're-enter childhood'. This idea goes far to explain role theory's facile linkage with the social phenomenon known as 'child-centredness' – that combination of conscientious empathy and aspiration that has dominated American pedagogy for the past decades – at first under the aegis of popular conditioning theory (behaviourism), later popular Freudianism. Today, however, the changed meaning of socialization itself is largely the work of role theorists who have emphasized the continuous, ongoing nature of social learning and role taking. They emphasize the changeful, adaptive aspects of role that are at odds with early childhood determinism or fixed developmental sequences. Socialization begins in childhood but does not end there.

Our dominant socialization theories bear in common the view that the young pass from 'egocentric' to 'sociocentric' behaviours (Piaget, Freud, Mead) and to the gradual differentiation of behaviour (through learning, role taking, or the vicissitudes of different psychosexual stages on life's way). Imitation or learning, identification and role taking are, broadly speaking, the favoured first principles of behaviourism, psychoanalysis, and sociology, respectively. Neither exclusive nor fully adequate as theories, they have been modified in different ways. In general, modification has followed debate upon three aspects of socialization theory: its generalizability from place to place (cross-cultural debate); its generalizability from social class to social class (comparative class data); its fixity or permanence (primary and secondary socialization).

First, the influence of anthropology on socialization theory

* See P. Aries, *Centuries of Childhood.*

and research has been enormous. Role theory is relatively open regarding matters of social setting and developmental sequence. Our personality theories are, by comparison, too close to our own habits and experiences to be broadly applicable. Freud's view of the family as 'the play within the play', the little society at home, was so important it could not be dismissed. In focusing on the family, however, it soon became evident that there could be no general theory of personality development, no general talk of the 'nature of man', no fixed sequences of psychosexual phases that contributed to the character of persons everywhere. What has endured is the Freudian notion of the primacy of the family; and what has resulted is intensive research into family and childhood because the family is the 'transmission belt' of culture, along with much argument about the meaning of 'primary' and 'secondary' institutions. The family is 'primary' because it comes first, but is its influence also the most enduring? Can we derive all other institutions from it – see the shape of the economic producer as well as the heavenly Father in the roles and images it provides? We shall not tarry over these points here because we return to them later on. Let us quickly summarize the argument against the 'pure personality theory' of the Freudians, according to which personality is a complex pattern of behaviours, begun in infancy, set in the course of childhood, and frozen into the character defences we all recognize as adulthood.

The social setting within which the person grows is the family. Are families alike? Yes and no. They show considerable variation by historical period, by region, by nation, by social class. When we move to areas outside European or American experience, the differences are so great we can only draw contrasts, not comparisons. We might say that the anthropologists injected a culture shock second only to that of Freud himself when he destroyed the myth of 'happy childhood'. They attacked the myth of a universal psychology based on instinct (fixed nature) and patriarchal power (fixed culture). In Freudian theory the power of the father is predicated upon the repression of everyone else, and Freud saw in sexual repression the core and substance of all power and repression. Given a different kinship system, a family in which the father is not all-powerful, what happens? Suppose the children do not live with their parents but rove about the village living with different kin? Or suppose, instead of sexual repression, children have freedom and independence from an early age? Suppose the role of women, institutional as well as sexual, so changes the kinds of bonds she has with her husband and children that we can no longer see the situation as like our own? What, then, happens to our theory of socialization with its requisite internalization – its repression and guilt and development of a superego to match one's parents?

We return it to its place of origin, of course. We limit its relevance in time and place. This limitation has been the consequence of anthropological work. Among the first questions raised was that of the matrilineal society, for example the case of the Trobriand Islands, cited by Malinowski. There the biological father hardly figures in the life of the child; it is the mother's brother who has authority because he provides for the kin in his own (mother's) lineage. The husband-father is friend and companion. Was an Oedipus complex visible in such a society, or the simultaneous repression and exaltation of women? Hardly. Child-training patterns were different too: feeding, toileting and sexual play appeared to occasion none of the conflicts that produce so many of our own 'complexes'.

Malinowski's *Sexual Life of Savages* was published in 1929. Thereafter, the study of comparative kinship systems and child-rearing methods brought to a full stop the idea of a universal personality theory. *Growing Up in New Guinea* or *Coming of Age in Samoa* were vastly different from any known family experiences in Western society. Personality developed, of course; the principle of development remained – its course, its sequence, its outcome had to be specified by time and place and circumstance.

Second, the case has hardly been different regarding socialization studies in our own society. Because of their origins in middle-class thought and middle-class models, considerable controversy has, from the beginning, characterized these researches. The long debate over 'right techniques' to produce 'strong superegos' was always imperilled by the implications for different class or ethnic or religious groups. Say what one will, the class studies inevitably aroused moralism and invidious comparison, and they centred on two dominant middle-class concerns: aggression and achievement. In general, though the findings were not always consistent, the studies could be summarized in terms of a permissive abundance-psychology of the middle class and a punitive deprivation-psychology of the lower class. This is not to suggest that the researchers gave their blessing to middle-class training patterns. To the contrary, their message could only dismay those who, with the best of intentions, thought that psychology might happily apply to life.

Is permissiveness a good thing? According to one interpretation of Freudian doctrine it might seem best to avoid conflicts in those areas (oral, anal and sexual) where life-lasting complexes form. Davis and Havighurst claimed from their studies that lower-class child-rearing practices were more lenient and casual in this respect than those of the middle class. They observed that this advantage did not equip them for getting on well in middle-class-dominated schools or middle-class ways of life. Later, opposite findings were claimed by Sears, Maccoby, and Levin: to be sure, the time and place were different (1957 as against 1946, and Boston, not Chicago samples), but with this study the permissiveness of middle-class training moved forward and the tolerance of the lower class backward. Some have maintained that the differences were because the middle class had, in the meanwhile, absorbed popular psychological doctrines and applied them.

The comparative virtues of negative and positive reinforcement have been argued for centuries. A consistent finding (one of the few consistencies throughout all the studies) is the preference for physical punishment among lower-class parents. It is, on every count, a negative mode. But can the

70

moral punitiveness of much middle-class training be called positive? Not the researchers, but others observed the methodical withdrawal of love and approval, the 'cultivation' of anxiety, the insidious promotion of competitiveness in the middle-class family. Who was least prepared for life: the hostile, aggressive lower-class boy or the 'middle-class male child with his neurosis'? Apropos the latter, Arnold Green remarked on not the 'growth' of personality but '. . . personality absorption . . . an emotional blanketing of the child, bringing about slavish dependence' (1953, p. 294).

Urie Bronfenbrenner (1961) once characterized the congruity of this pattern with contemporary role requirements in suggesting that middle-class socialization techniques 'have the effect of undermining capacities for initiative and independence' and breed 'conforming and anxious' types rather than 'enterprising and self-sufficient' ones. Whichever way we look at the problem, personality did not emerge as a spontaneous and independent force to be posed against 'the role structure'.

Meanwhile, rather little attention was paid to separate surveys into the relationship between child-training practice and apparent outcome (Orlansky, 1949; Sewell, 1952). Both cast doubt on the apparent validity of psychoanalytic principles outside the clinic; both failed to find evidence for the predicted relationships that are taken for granted in all the child-rearing studies. Orlansky indicated how largely inconclusive was the evidence for the supposed superiority of breast feeding ('there is no linear correlation between length of breast feeding and any major aspect of personality', such as security or behaviour problems), for 'weaning trauma' (no experimental data), for thumb-sucking (available studies indicated that oral deprivation did not invariably result in habitual thumb-sucking – nor when thumb-sucking does occur can it necessarily be attributed to oral deprivation), motor restraint ('evidence suggests that where children are accustomed to such restraints as swaddling or the cradle board, they do not experience it as frustration'), and, as for the anal character, only 'fragmentary and inadequate' studies exist to lend support to the supposed relation between sphincter training and such traits as stubbornness, rigidity, cruelty and orderliness.

For sociologists the major interest in socialization studies has always centred on the process of internalization and, by derivation, through what techniques social necessity is converted into private duty and desire. It is, therefore, the appearance of conscience or superego or 'generalized other' that has been of first theoretical importance. According to personality theory, conscience is established very early, and the primary models are those of the family. Role theory stands in agreement with this principle, and many current doctrines interweave the internalization of role (taking the role of the other) with the introjected parental figures of Freudian theory. The identification with and introjection of parental authority that forms the superego, however, is a more grim and formidable process than the benign growth of G. H. Mead's 'generalized other'. Again, the very elaboration of the Freudian theory of internalization has led to numerous difficulties in interpreting either classes or cultures different from the original model. We may follow the problem at some length because it has brought to present crisis the whole socialization theory.

In the studies of social class in our own society, it has long been supposed that the crux of lower-class 'failure' was caused by inadequate superego formation (internalization). Very often this failure comes from the absence of the father, and the dominance of the mother determines a failure of masculine identity and, in turn, prepares the way for compensatory masculine aggression that is nourished by the lower-class gang or peer group. On the other hand, even if both the father and the mother are present, there is most likely a failure of internalization, because the quality of lower-class life and way of relating prevents 'object-cathexis' or 'identification'. The lower-class mother (it is said) is distant, punitive, unloving; the lower-class father is harsh, punitive and forbidding. Controls are never internalized, according to this theory, because the techniques of training remain external and primitive. To internalize we must experience love, for love makes us feel guilt whereas punishment merely gives us pain.

Of course, the theory has been sharply criticized; it rests on a bounty of doctrine and a slim hold of fact; and it perhaps deserves harsher criticism than it has actually received. In passing we might note, for example, that Miller and Swanson (1968) found, as virtually all investigators have, that physical punishment was the preferred disciplinary technique in their lower-class sample. They did not find a lack of conscience or internalization:

Judging from the data, boys in the middle class do not differ significantly from boys in the working class in the severity of their guilt about disobedience, death wishes or stealing. At first glance, this result seemed to contradict reports that boys in the working class do not internalize standards as adequately as do boys in the middle class. Hence, the sons of manual labourers find it easy to disobey authorities, to express all kinds of hostile wishes and to steal. Our data certainly indicate that they fight more than their counterparts in the middle class. Then why do we not find differences in the standards of the two classes? Behaviour may vary with socio-economic level, not because of contrasting standards but because of differences in the capacity to live up to them. . . . Boys may feel compelled to steal or be disobedient to save face with their friends. Their anti-social behaviour, however, does not mean that they suffer any less than middle class boys from the pressures of internalized standards.

According to the doctrinaires of internalization theory, however, the failure of the superego is made evident by the derelict behaviour and such derelictions lead back to superego failure. There is yet more. A superego failure not only spells a moral lapse (thus accounting for juvenile delinquency as well as later non-achievement), it signifies an intellectual one. No object-identification occurs; the capacity to be objective fails to develop; the lower-class child remains stupefied for life. He cannot learn properly his tasks in school; no more can he master complex objectives later on. Sometimes the comparative linguistic habits of different classes (B. Bern-

73

stein) have been adduced as supporting evidence to a generalized psychic deprivation.

The theory is not a pleasant one, to be sure. After all, we expect deprivation to show an ugly face. The difficulty is not that but its implicit smugness: it bears a certain resemblance to the once established notion that the poor deserved to be poor because they were too stupid and unenergetic to make themselves rich; just so, the lower classes fall into place because, unfortunately, they lack the right superegos. Two counter-arguments have been made, one of which we have presented above: it denies the alleged absence of conscience. The other argument has to do with the priority of things social versus things psychic: until lower-class life conditions change, we cannot expect much change in superegos.

Of course, the whole array of arguments surrounding internalization again turns upon the questions of early determinism and psychological fate and presents grave difficulties for our educational enterprise. Can 'secondary' institutions, like our schools, train and prepare these backward citizens, or are they predeterminately fated by their early childhood? Should the state remove them from their families and save them for society, as some have gone so far as to propose?

We have pursued this long argument because it raises harsh questions and sharp issues. A strict personality theory resting on doctrines of 'early childhood determinacy' and the 'failure of internalization' has, in the hands of its proponents, not been content to stay within the confines of mere theory. The uses to which such personality theorists put their theory have included policy proposals squarely in the middle of politics. There they have provoked debate and aroused anger and resentment. In America this anger is particularly the case because, for generations, backward and benighted Europeans, unaided by guides to child-training and in doubtful grip of intact superegos, have managed to 'raise themselves up' by beneficial cooperation of an expanding economy and fairly good luck.

Hence there is a 'politics of personality', and whether we like it or not, it intrudes upon our researches. Currently it appears that changes in American society – in class and politics and race – have outstripped our ability to formulate meaningful questions about early childhood. The problems that figured so prominently in the research of yesterday – the search for the origins of dependency and achievement, frustration and aggression, punitiveness and permissiveness – are cast into shadow by the march of events themselves. Thus, major shifts in the economy that we call the opportunity structure force a rethinking of what used to be termed the achievement orientation of different ethnic groups. Was it their motivation that mattered or their being in the right place at the right time? And how are we to explain the very rapidly developed achievement motivations of American Negroes, hitherto regarded as bereft of good mother figures as well as strong fatherly ones? Is it possible that the civil rights movement has overcome their oppressive childhood as well as forced open the golden gate of opportunity? The shifting scene no longer accommodates the relevance of childhood; nor can we demonstrate its lasting determinancy. Events change; so do we.

Yet for a long time, the relative openness of the role-taking principle has shown certain advantages over tightly developed personality theories. The 'generalized other' can be as authoritarian as the superego, provided these are the kinds of role models that have, in fact, been presented to us. It does not *have* to be. Again, in role theory, too, socialization begins in childhood, but it does not end there. In theory, at least, we grow and we change, and we are not necessarily compelled to repeat our early experiences unless our later social roles support our initial passivity or submissiveness or aggression.

Moreover, role theory has proved a more congenial teaching for expanding and changing societies. It involves the notion of continuous socialization and dovetails with the needs of a technically changing economy for persons ready and able to shoulder a life programme of 'continuing education'. Much more important has been the gradual extension of the concept of socialization to include role learning at any period of the life cycle. Thus the role concept came to absorb all life's discontinuities that psychoanalytic theory either neglected or discounted. It is true that for a time these forms were assimilated as 'secondary' socializations, the family remaining 'primary', but this awkward distinction has all but lost its usefulness. In the meantime, the literature of socialization has grown to include a variety of career indoctrinations (the making of scientists, lawyers, physicians), group identifications (the soldier, the corporation man), critical experiences of desocialization and resocialization (the moral career of the mental patient, the disengagement of the aged, the brainwashing of the POW).* Role theory accommodates our real social experience that has lost its character of predictable development out of known childhood sources and presents instead a picture of discontinuity, of abrupt taking on as well as putting behind different roles and that requires an active, willing facilitation of person to objective demands without regret or reminiscence.

The unforeseen timeliness of G. H. Mead's theory was the new kind of conscience called the 'generalized other', sociable and capable of infinite extension. Properly speaking, in role theory, socialization never ends. Its longevity is coextensive with life itself.

Third, the distinction between primary and secondary socialization continues to present difficulties. We have followed various phases of criticism and rethinking in socialization theory. We have come to its turning point in problems surrounding internalization. In what way do we incorporate role models? How fixed and lasting is that incorporation? How stable and immutable are our role experiences? Generally, internalization refers to our early learning, and it is often synonymous with 'primary socialization'. Are not our later roles also internalized? What is meant by their 'secondariness'?

* A comprehensive survey of gradual shifts in socialization research – not so much to adult aspects as to the gradual incorporation of role theory to familial relationships, adolescence and the like – may be found in W. Sewell's 'Some Recent Developments in Socialization Theory and Research' (1963).

Since sociologists are supposed naturally to be more concerned about secondary socialization, they have occasionally posed the question of the relation between the two types. If, as research suggests, the primary type is primary in the sense of earliest or first but is not permanently determining behaviour, we have to temper expectations of its predictive capacity. The child may be 'father to the man' but be as estranged from his own childhood as from his own father. Critical stages in adulthood, adaptations, turning points, present situation may prove much more predictive of behaviour now. Where do they fit in?

The most obvious solution would suggest that personalities are something like the societies in which they grow: the stability and continuity of the one must have much to do with the stability of the other. Childhood experience may well prove predictive of adult patterns where there are no marked discontinuities, where early preparation actually relates to later experience, where the family holds its own. But the old functions and powers of the family are largely lost to 'secondary' institutions in all societies we call modern.

This elemental fact seems scarcely to be acknowledged in the literature on socialization. Primary and secondary socialization involve a host of qualitative differences. First, there is the matter of priority in time. 'First' and 'earliest' give parental dominance a running start; but there is more. The hapless dependency of infancy provides the ground for that emotional cathexis Freud saw as the psychological ground for power in the family and society as well. Hence, there has lingered a conviction that 'primary' means more than earliest: its affective quality and its intensity mean that it is embedded in the person. Thus, Brim (in J. Clausen, 1968) calls primary and secondary socialization different types – the first still immovably there, whatever our later experiences may be; the second, external conformist, adaptive to current requirements and the situation of the moment. The quite different work of Peter Berger and Thomas Luckmann (1967) follows a similar course. Primary socialization is the first induction into society but it is also the most important: all secondary socialization has to resemble the earliest, for the earliest has provided the definitions for all social experience. Our earliest experiences were emotionally charged learning and therefore presumably unforgettable.

This familiar combination of psychoanalytic and role theory provides a current formula, but there are difficulties. The large literature on secondary socialization is not just a modification of the original doctrine but implies the significant social change that has made us reassess what is 'prior' and 'permanent'. The family has lost to state and economy virtually all power; it is left with overcharged emotional significance, sentiment, and symbolic vestment. The difficulty for social psychology is that such meanings provide insufficient guidelines. The discontinuities are often glaring, and we find ourselves referring to secondary institutions experiences that are in no sense secondary, and calling primary those identifications that have lost the capacity to furnish an identity.

Current debates suggest that the problem of stability – the primary source of personality traced through the life history as the 'core' of the 'essential' person – is not easily solved by traditional personality theories. Provisionally, we have to say that such stability may occur; more often we must qualify our statement and look for sources of balance, integration, consistency or predictability elsewhere. As the quality of modern life has changed, so has the person. The sources of his personality are as multiple and complex as his life history.

The notion that personality is deeply embedded, that our later experiences are secondary and superficial, that roles are merely taken on and cast off to suit the occasion, has resulted in quite divergent views. It may lead us to discount personality altogether and view social life dramatically as a continuous show; or it may cause us to hold insistently to the inner self, the man nobody knows. Neither view describes why individual conflict and change relate as regularly as they do to ongoing social change. Were we mere role takers, change would occasion no conflict; were we 'to our own selves true', change would never present itself as a possibility.

Old self–new selves is not a drama that lies deep within us – it is an altogether more ordinary experience.

Perhaps the best formulation we have had of the problem is one that Erich Fromm made long ago in *Fear of Freedom* when his task was to explain the stupendous change of social revolution. In the face of objective social change, he observed, old norms and patterns no longer do; new models are espoused because they more adequately match and interpret new experience. These are, in turn, absorbed and passed on as a 'tradition of the new'. We well know that such absorption can be very rapid indeed, that selves can be remade in less than a generation's time, that the long journey through the superego is not a necessary one at all. Social revolution is but one example, however, and suggests that social life is not always revolving, generational conflicts are not always brewing, group claims are not shifting, inventions and innovations are not seducing us from the ways of our fathers.

We may, in conclusion, review the general cultural context within which individuality develops and against which all doctrines of personality have emerged. 'Socialization' describes the process through which mind and self develop as forms of consciousness within a specific social and historical milieu. In role theory, this symbolic elaboration is built upon a basic theory of language and communication. Still, the linguistic facts on which it is based are as general as language itself while a similar individualization is not. Evidently, as a theory many of its features are specific to our own time and place. How is it to be adapted?

Generally, for comparative purposes, the more content-free our categories for interpreting behaviour in other societies, the better. Critically, we have no theory of socialization that can stand upon a universal psychology of self and character, and the relatively objective descriptions of role (as function, performance or requirement) are, in this respect, advantageous. Because the basic process and mechanics of growing up are not everywhere the same, we have to separate role and self theory. As a general learning principle, its applicability is

D   79

clear enough; but in so far as it details an inward-outward process of mind and self, its description evidently remains partial
to our own experience. The fact is we do very poorly in
understanding societies other than our own or the consciousness of persons very different from ourselves. In its external
sense the role concept is broadly useful. It describes the social
person, who he is and what he does; it avoids assumptions of
a kind of universal selfishness of self and steers clear of
forms of inwardness that have demonstrable reference only
to our own experience. The visions of mystics everywhere,
from India to North America, may like men's dreams be
alike as psychic phenomena. Their meaning, their interpretation, their experience is not. We still stand largely outside
that experience, it is not ours; we can only describe it
objectively.

We may be reminded here of the kinds of problems re-
current in an ethnography that drifted into philosophical
anthropology. From Lévy-Bruhl's 'primitive mentality' to
contemporary notions of the 'savage mind' (Lévi-Strauss),
we are presented with the problem of categorical differences.
While we safely assume that types of logic, forms of awareness, or consciousness itself must be related to social structure,
and that meanings must be communicated in ways not wholly
variant from our own, light is yet to be cast on the direction
and path of these known differences. Individualization is not
the problem – understanding its absence is. Forms of consciousness that are not accompanied by self-consciousness
are all but unimaginable to us. At that point the distinctions
that we draw are almost as automatic as they are categorical.
Preliterate or savage societies are not characterized by our
consciousness at all; but neither are societies outside of the
main traditions of the West; nor, until very recently, were
classes within Western societies seen as similarly endowed.
We may call to mind here the many references to under-
privileged classes as lower orders, halfway between savage
and civilized, that typified social commentaries hardly a century ago.

Differentiation of the self has received different explanations but is ultimately referable to social structure, whether, as in Freudian theory, we find a mirroring and internalization of authoritarian family structure (the superego) or internalization of roles (Mead's 'generalized other'). In contrast, structural anthropological theories are not social-psychological but render abstract forms of consciousness as counterparts (and often reflections of) social structure and organization, using for their examples basic linguistic contrasts and oppositions and simply categories of difference. Presumably the savage mind experiences these directly and absorbs them uncomplicatedly. Typical social-psychological explanation would, in contrast, involve reference to this all but vanished savage social world as one of limited roles and fixed role ascriptions.

Social-psychologically, we can relate mind to socialization and social structure, as Mead did in indicating that in caste societies, for example, with their typical restrictions, the development of the 'generalized other' or common attitudes was limited, as was the full development of the self. Modern functional differences open up common roles; caste and status societies restrict them. Precluding multiple and common relations, they preclude also the differentiation of the self. Further elaboration of these points may be found in Gerth's and Mills's *Character and Social Structure* (pp. 99–106) where full development of the self is also characterized in terms of roles and role choices. Beyond this development, emphasis is placed on the fact that the individual emerges just because as group accountability (kin, caste, status) decreases voluntary choice increases.

This last aspect – the relative weight and value of the individual *per se* – has been emphasized in Ullmann's work (1966) on medieval comparisons. The low standing of the individual, manifested in what he calls the 'rule of anonymity' and corporate responsibility and expressed institutionally in diverse ways, he takes as a characteristic feature of the Middle Ages. The question for the historian is how, from that setting, individualization grew. Observing the absorption of the individual by society. Ullmann said, 'I can only testify to my own annoyance when I come across a work of art or of literature or of documentation which so successfully hides its author.' He adds:

What do we know of the men who conceived and executed some of the finest architectural works still the marvel of even this highly sophisticated generation? Who wrote this or that tract which often started a new line of thought or even a school? . . . What was the head of the chancery at this or that time drafting this or that decree or law with its beautifully arranged Arenga? [pp. 33–4].

Our annoyance as well as difficulty in understanding that social experience need not be sifted through the individual defines the major boundaries of our social psychology. In short, so strong is our own feeling that we do not see its essential irrelevance to an epoch different from our own. Sometimes men dream themselves into other epochs and periods and try imaginatively to recapture them; but they must admire from a distance; they cannot 'live' it.

Far from sharing the sentiments Ullmann expresses above, the American philosopher, Charles Sanders Peirce, held the medievalists quite close to an intellectual ideal:

Think of the spirit in which Duns Scotus must have worked, who wrote his thirteen volumes in folio in a style as condensed as the most condensed parts of Aristotle, before the age thirty-four. Nothing is more striking in either of the great intellectual products of that age than the complete absence of self-conceit on the part of artist or philosopher. That anything of value can be added to his sacred and catholic work by its having the smack of individuality about it, is what he has never conceived. His work is not designed to embody *his* ideas, but the universal truth; there will not be one thing in it, however minute, for which you will not find that he has his authority; and whatever originality emerges is of that inborn kind which so saturates a man that he cannot perceive it. The individual feels his own worthlessness in comparison with his task, and does not dare to introduce his vanity into the doing of it. Then there is no machine-work, no unthinking repetition about the thing. Every part is worked out for itself as a separate problem, no matter how analogous it may be in general to another part. And no matter how small and hidden a detail may be, it has been conscientiously studied, as though it were intended for the eye of God [in W. B. Gallie (1966), p. 58].

We might well place in a similar context the attraction of forms of Eastern mysticism. Then the aim is not to find or express the self, but to free it, to dissociate it from all relations with mind and body. The contrasts that have been drawn are especially interesting because East and West alike 'discovered' the self but with completely different consequence. Subjectivity can be suppressed or it can be stressed; one can work at detaching the self so that there remain only 'liberated spirits that are egoless', as Regamey (1968) has put it, or there can be attached to the self the highest rational and spiritual faculties, giving us the familiar ego psychologies of the West.

Such differences in attitude towards the mind are easier to describe than to explain. While they are systematically related to differences in religious and political and legal institutions, presumably they are also intimately related to role learning and role experience. If fixed social forms give way, so too does the fixity of roles. Instead of being bound to particular ones, the person is free to take on or try out different roles. Then the self can be conceived as a 'testing' or 'realizing' itself in this world. The person, like the social structure of which he is a part, is an historical product too. He reflects his society: he becomes similarly differentiated; he develops 'selfhood'. But recent social psychologies complete the refraction in different ways: for some, the area left to self, once role description is completed, is slim indeed; some stratify the person, some flatten him into a plateau of roles and corresponding images; some appraise personal histories and unique experiences, others do not; virtually none preserve, in original form, Mead's formless and idealized 'I'. Hence, the degree of autonomy depends upon the writer's relocating its source. Different definitions of self and society are summarized in Table 5.1.

Gerth and Mills ascribe greatest importance to the fact that the self-image develops and changes and becomes the basis for

Table 5.1. Theoretical Conceptions of Self and Society

	INDIVIDUAL PERSONALITY	MEDIATING PROCESS	SOCIETY
Social behaviourism	'I' and 'me' (unique weighting of roles)	role-learning and role-taking	'generalized other', the community
Behaviourism	unique conditioning history	learning and role-learning	reward structure
Interactionist	'self' and personality (durable integration of roles and responses to them)	role-learning and role-taking	institutional order
Social system	personality 'system'	roles	social system
Personality (psycho-analytic)	psychic structure: id-ego-superego (characteristic 'defences')	ego functions (resolution of psycho-social conflicts)	authority structure

accepting or rejecting, ignoring or expanding various roles; we cannot describe what precedes or lies outside of social experience. But Goffman assumes virtual correspondence of self-image and role; a self is taken on as a role, is 'stepped into', and autonomy is an illusion. For Parsons, the personality system is highly stratified, but it functions in such close interlocking relation to the social system (roles) that voluntary or autonomous behaviours are those falling outside the system – we must look for them in areas of dislocation, alienation and deviation (where, however, the terms voluntary or autonomous are quite irrelevant).

Generally, the restatement of personality in terms of objective role and subjective responses to that role gives us the key terms of social behaviourism. More generally, we can say that the way the self is projected and the way in which it is experienced are derived from society and social relationships. But how various are the portrayals of the self! There was once a sovereign self to match the sovereign state; and out of a hierarchical and class-conscious society there emerged conceptions of the stratified self. For our own time, there has emerged the divided or fragmented self. Even more recently we have had presented the 'transparent self', the spectre of which was raised by Orwell's *1984*, its bowdlerization by group therapies, its political truth made clear by the totalitarian conception of the thoroughly 'social self'.* How well we may remember Koestler's hero in *Darkness at Noon*: 'The Party denied the free will of the individual – and at the same time it exacted his willing self-sacrifice. It denied his capacity to choose between two alternatives – and at the same time it demanded that he should constantly choose the right one.' The victim is urged to tell the whole truth, but under these conditions there is but one truth. By definition, self-disclosure is simply public condemnation. We may rightly be wary, therefore, of preachments for self-disclosure. Disclosure is a good thing, we are told, because it 'opens' the self. Only the guilty, the anxious and the fearful have something to hide; only the weak need shelter and concealment (Jourard). Indeed we might agree to all of this and yet maintain that precisely because of it, protection must be guaranteed the one who discloses. The psychology of breaking through the character armour or of working through defences can only be valid if the person is, in turn, defended through privacy, privileged communication or professional ethics. Otherwise he is merely exposed.

The social self is extroverted and adaptable, presumably untroubled by differences between private and public

* The references are to S. Jourard, *The Transparent Self* (1964), and to E. Berne's social games. See also R. Bauer's *The New Man in Soviet Psychology* (1952).

exposure because the very category of privacy is obviated; and such a self is uncomplicated by problems of depth or disclosure because participation is complete and open. Thus far, the optimum social conditions for the emergence of such a self are wanting.

6

Role Analysis

IN point of theory, the great advantage of G. H. Mead's teaching was to root personality in society, to relocate mind or consciousness within social process, and to unify mind, self and society through role taking and symbol learning. Social behaviourism in theory was rather different from social behaviourism in practice, however, and what had been unified in theory was in practice put asunder by the exigencies of research techniques. It was in the theory and practice of small group research that role theory came to have its most obvious applications.

We do not need to recapitulate here the diverse sources of the small group movement that was well nourished by psychological as well as social theories, nor to see special significance in the resurgence of the small group through the supposed primariness of the primary group. The importance of the small group pales before the fact of sheer expediency in a milieu that places enormous premiums on the experimental, not in life but in the laboratory, and on practice, not in the laboratory but in life. The small group was a manageable unit and lent itself to the common language of role analysis (which came to dominate it) and to the practice of experimental research.

How do we capture the social process as Mead described it? We know, because he described in detail and in example, what is meant by interaction, significant gesture and symbol, and socialization via role playing. But suppose we demand evidence beyond the merely observed and experienced; or, as we say of workable theory, suppose we require of it a capacity not simply to draw together hitherto disparate data but to furnish a basis for continuing inquiry and research? At first glance Mead's theory would seem more suggestive than susceptible to formulations of an experimental sort. Its descriptions were apt but elusive, its language down to earth but fluid and mobile, its data seemingly fleeting and transitory. The very ongoingness of the act, and the shifting ground of role taking and role playing, suggest at once the difficulties of the social process standing still enough at any given point for us to measure as well as describe it. Yet, with interesting consequences, measuring the social process has been precisely the achievement of this era of research in social psychology. There was, of course, a price: vivacity and ongoingness gave way to fixed descriptions of role, function and position; interaction was reduced to measurable communicative exchanges; and self was hardly distinguishable from image – we are all those appearances we make, we are as others see us. In fact, one of the most frequently cited tests of interaction hypotheses deriving from Mead consists of comparing image and self-image in order to establish their congruity (Miyamoto and Dornbusch, 1956). The image has become the frozen form in which Mead's theory of self, born of social process, is captured and vindicated. By now a sizeable body of research on self, self-image and appraisal of self and others is taken as confirmation of his theory.

If, instead of Mead's analysis, we emphasize the consequences of it, the transition from theory to practice is clear and simple. A focus on social process, act or interaction implies that we direct our attention outwards to objective analysis and descriptive recount. We forsake discussion of what men are and look at what they do. Once this basic reorientation occurred, the elaboration of methods for observing, counting and measuring behaviours followed apace. The complete externalization of the social act eliminated the troublesome, introspective parts of Mead's theory (which were siphoned off as studies of self-conception, image and identity). The culmination of this transition may be seen in the true social behaviourism of Robert Bales's *Interaction Process Analysis* – essentially a content analysis of communicative acts in a group setting.

We may remark that difficulties of coding and quantification are but one aspect of this analysis. A more interesting consequence is that we are led to qualitative appraisals only by way of quantitative differences derived from the coding itself. The basic differentiation of function in this analysis of group process has crystallized about two basic classifications that hark back to the coding categories. Here, it will be recalled, communications were regarded either as emotional (expressive) or informational (task-solving). This basic point of departure for the analysis of meaning is, of course, long familiar from the literature of positivism and semantics. It subsequently dominated small-group research as a readily available code and technique and tended to channel small-group thinking along its own lines. Contrast should be emphasized here, however, for alternative coding procedures have been used with rather different consequences. The categories used by Bion (therapy groups) and adapted by D. Stock and H. Thelen (1958) provide for simultaneous scoring of task-emotional communications. In this dual scoring procedure, different proportions of work-emotionality occur in different groups (and at different phases of group development, as Bales also found); but neither the theory behind the coding nor the results lead to the clear division of principle Bales found.

Let us compare the categories. Bales's (1950) list includes the following:

1. Shows solidarity
2. Shows tension release
3. Shows agreement
4. Gives suggestion
5. Gives opinion
6. Gives information

7. Asks for information
8. Asks for opinion
9. Asks for suggestion
10. Shows disagreement
11. Shows tension
12. Shows antagonism

Such a classification is sufficiently general that it can be used for many different purposes, as it has been. Acts can be scored for their positive or negative qualities, for example, or for problem solving, or for tension-release attempts; or only certain acts may be scored in order to determine flow of information, so that items 1, 2 and 3 at one end, and items 10, 11 and 12 at the other can be eliminated. At the same time, we are made aware of possible scoring problems just by reading down the list. The categories are not mutually exclusive, and especially the 'emotional' acts (shows solidarity, antagonism, disagreement) are not necessarily separable from the 'instrumental' ones (gives suggestion or information). There are, after all, ways of giving a suggestion and asking for information: some compliment and some complement; some are nice and some are not, and some are neutral. We may suppose that much of the difficulty was ordinarily disguised by narrow and specific definition of the research problem. Often, how groups progress toward a decision or move toward equilibrium could exclude qualitative aspects in favour of quantitative ones and then return later to qualitative problems. The classification lends itself to this procedure by the ready separation of its items. The only difficulty is that in following it we should divide every single communicative act into its instrumental and emotional aspect, whereas in ordinary communication the two are indivisible.

Suppose a quite different assumption is made. Then, as Bion has done (and Stock and Thelen, in turn), emotional and task items would not appear as separate categories in a list like Bales's; instead, every individual act is scored for its emotional and its task aspect – or to use Bion's terms, 'work and emotionality'. If this is the case, we are likely to get scrambled effects and mixed distributions; it would be difficult for task and emotional items to be opposed and separated because from the beginning they have been scored together.

Bion called the emotional components that mattered to him 'pairing, dependency, fight-flight', which appeared in some typical combinations with work to give characteristic group descriptions; they also gave descriptions of individual performance. Because it was never assumed that one could really separate work and emotional aspects or that some individuals were specialized in their communications, it seems never to have been discovered that some individuals in the group were 'task' and some 'emotional' specialists. It may be noted that, in part of the research reported, there were individual subtypes who were clearly recognized to have leadership needs and made active bids for leadership in groups (Stock and Thelen, pp. 111–12). It was also found that more hostility was directed toward one of these (as Bales also showed). It would be quite impossible to categorize the subtype as either task or emotional leader, however, and we are not surprised to learn that he was truly a medley of things.

The most immediate and significant consequence of Bales's dual principle was that it became the basis for all subsequent thinking about small-group role differentiation. Thus, the qualitative analysis of small-group roles (tied to two types of communication) remained notably primitive.

There is no acknowledged way to render a complete analysis of the social act. We learn much simply by counting interchanges (the interaction rate). Direction of communication (who talks to whom) requires interpretation, however, and has therefore been used as a criterion for quite various purposes (for example, centrality of leadership, as well as deviation). The search for an equilibrium principle has perhaps been the most ardent as well as superfluous of sociological tasks. Here, it may be observed, a sensitive analysis of any kind must depend strongly on the purposes and nature of the group. The essential purposelessness of many experimental groups simplifies classification and coding difficulties but at the same time reveals little new information. We mean by 'purposelessness' that experimental groups are often composed of student subjects whose entry into the experimental situation for pay or fun, as the case may be, along with the contrived arrangements of the experimenter, makes of the experimental group a species unlike any found elsewhere in social life. What, then, was discovered about roles and the role-taking person in the small experimental group?

The Small Group and the Personality Principle

We have pointed to the way in which role conceptions generally redefine the person in terms of what he does. The person is really the sum of his roles or social performances. But in small-group research the problem of personality has often been retained – sometimes as a way of explaining un-understood variance and sometimes simply in deference to old theories. Perhaps the most common formulation is that the behaviour of the person is to be understood not just by expectations and role definitions (imposed from outside) but as an expression of self (from within). This seemingly plausible proposition has, for most sociologists, appeared quite unprofitable to pursue. Roles themselves vary greatly in the degree of freedom permitted to the person, in emotional expressiveness, in style, and in adherence or departures from conventional norms. In practice, then, it seems almost impossible to isolate 'personality' from 'role'.

Moreover, in approaching this material, the laboratory culture is likely to present itself as a problem. The abstract, pure situation of the small group has created the artifact customarily identified in the literature as the small group whose only uniform properties are its unidentifiability with any natural group (and typically with any other experimental group since variations in size, purpose and nature make each unique) and its controllability. Nonetheless, for comparative purposes, it has evolved aims, problems and a vocabulary of its own – not least important of which is a distinctive role vocabulary.

The most striking fact is that despite seemingly good conditions for exploring problems of personality (small size, limited aims, strict controls), its narrow functionalism has led to a miniature social-systems approach that is intrinsically inimical to the study of personality. In part this is caused by an interest in quantifying all observations, in part, to the inescapable limits of coding procedures designed for simplicity and clarity, and therefore, in turn, to the narrow delimitation of roles. Hence, a decided role stereotypy has emerged, among which we may identify leadership roles (dual-task, emotional), the deviant, and the slider. What, then, can be said about the relation of any of these roles to the problem of personality?

We may point initially to the almost insuperable difficulties of matching pure personality types, as they are ordinarily conceived, to particular roles. Thus the possible congruency of personality characteristics to role demands has to centre on particular traits. The essential circularity of the proof derives from the culturally given fact that we cannot separate personality traits from role demands. Whether we assume, in theory, that persons with particular traits are attracted to certain roles or that role occupancy creates traits hardly matters. From either the standpoint of pure personality or pure role theory, particular traits are required for any enactment. The only significant issue, therefore, arises when particular traits are taken as indicative of a type or a complex – for example, the use of an F-score (authoritarianism) or an anxiety measure – whose interpretations irradiate controversy. We should, in short, expect correlations between certain group functions and specific traits wherever a particular trait is, by definition, a role requirement. The dominance or ascendancy of task leaders should not be difficult to confirm – it is merely redundant. But dominance or ascendancy may or may not also possess measurable anxiety or authoritarianism – traits they may also share with others.

In discussing these problems we merely accentuate many that role theory sought to cast into oblivion, for if we begin with the assumption that it is behaviour we are primarily interested in, and the comparison of behaviours from group situation to situation, questions of personality are not relevant to our main purposes. We may more profitably assume that if a person functions in a given role, he must possess the trait requisite to it; and the question of trait correlates is not one of durable significance to group research.

Of the few approaches to this problem, Borgatta's (1961, 1964) attempts to confirm personality and role congruency are perhaps the most notable. In his role-playing experiments, persons were assigned roles varying in assertiveness (assertive, submissive and emotional), and their recorded scores (using interaction process categories) were correlated with their original assertiveness scores. The relationships, while confirmed, were 'only mild'.

More typical and frequent of the uses of personality in small-group research is its displacement from the individual to the group level. Here, the tendency has been to call 'personality' any individual psychological measure imposed upon participants in a group experiment. The use of the F-scale (authoritarian personality) or of diagnostic Rorschach and TAT scores as personality measures to be correlated with interaction rate have been common procedures (Hare, 1962, pp. 178–90). The result seems actually to be a negation of the principle of individuality, however, for instead of establishing unique or unusual effects, or individual contributions and influences, group means on particular traits have been correlated with group performances. Far from indicating individual personality factors, the measured traits become standardized for the group and not the individual, but 'group personality' marches forward.

If groups may be said to have a 'personality', so appears to go the reasoning, it is only because the individuals who compose them do. This group personality can be demonstrated by varying the composition of groups, i.e. sorting them by personality test scores. But an inherent difficulty with these demonstrations (and there are a number of them) is that groups differ even when they are not 'controlled' for the personality factor, or at least this is true in real life, and in the absence of control groups, we have really only shown that we can get different scores from different personality test groups, compared with each other but never matched against untested groups.

Haythorn's (1955, 1956) research served as the model, and over many years it has conserved the purest psychology of personality: groups composed of persons high on various attitudes, needs or traits display, so it is averred, behaviours consistent with their member traits. The difficulties of this proposition have emerged conspicuously in attempts to correlate F-scale scores with different groups' performances.* But even with less controversial measures, the design of the studies cannot inspire confidence.

More recently, a large and ambitious research, similarly dedicated to demonstrating the relationship between personality structure and group functioning, posed the problem in similar terms (Tuckman, 1964). Groups were sorted according to personality type (determined by personality test), and their subsequent performance was then interpreted in personality terms. Essentially four group structures (of different 'personality') were compared in a game-playing group performance. Here again the interchangeability of individual and group 'personality' means that emphasis can fall on either group theory or personality theory. Interpretations vary with the researcher. But it seems essential if we wish to demonstrate the difference between individual personality and the group that we do not simply compare 'personality groups' and interpret their performance, but match them along the way – presumably with groups not subjected to personality tests or with groups randomly composed from the standpoint of personality characteristics.

It is probably true that one can create a group personality

* On their consistently inconsistent findings, see McGrath and Altman, *Small Group Research* (1966), p. 57, who observe that 'in general, authoritarian attitudes show very little relationship to most interaction behaviours and inconsistent relationships with performance on tasks of various types'. Like others, these authors comment on the paucity of personality data here and observe that the 'influence of personal characteristics on group functioning is an area worthy of further study'.

by controlling the personalities of those who compose it, but this condition is neither necessary nor sufficient to account for group differences or even for group atmospheres. Here experimental evidence only adds to historical controversy, for, as Lewin, Lippitt and White (1939) early demonstrated, different group atmospheres can be created, irrespective of the personality characteristics of members, simply by varying styles of leadership. Much small-group research is, in this respect, devoted to the proposition that groups vary by reason of diverse situational and interaction patterns (for example, power or participation) in all of which personality, because it has not been controlled, is assumed to have random effects.

Generally, then, the most conspicuous feature of this group research is the evanescence of the principle of personality from the person and its relocation in the group – where we either do not immediately recognize it or, recognizing it, must also acknowledge that it has acquired a very different meaning. The metamorphoses that lead from individual characteristics to differential group composition to group ethos or atmosphere are not subtle but gradual. Moreover, the possible sources of group differences are numerous so that pattern or process, morale or participatory behaviour, as well as personality, have been treated as a basis for differentiating groups – each as a kind of endowment of character or personality to the group.*

Amidst this confusion, the grave difficulties of separating role from person and person from role could be deliberately avoided, or some of its attendant interest could be focused instead on the intensive analysis of particular roles. Curiously enough, role differentiation itself, as a focal point for scrutiny, has remained stereotyped. For research nourished upon the theoretical field of role specialization, the lack of individua-

* See, for example, McGrath's and Altman's statements, by no means atypical of discussions of the problem of personality in the small group: 'Personality properties should be studied with respect to the composition of the group', one problem; but, 'It is probably not the presence or absence of member anxiety *per se* but rather the pattern of anxiety among group members that makes a difference', a quite different problem (op. cit., p. 57).

tion remains conspicuous. We may truly speak here of role stereotypy: leaders and followers, deviants and conformists, high and low communicators, yielders and non-yielders, point, like the 'stars' and 'isolates' of early sociometry, to a social universe frozen in its role casting and quite unenriched by capacious role taking. We may, then, remain unconvinced that this is an adequate depiction of even the smallest of social worlds; or we may regard it as inevitable that the individual and the distinctive get lost in measuring group process. The fact is that roles were differentiated as we acquired measures for them; as mere emblems for the study of group process, performance, interaction rate, or mode of participation, their 'personal' aspects disappeared. Role was defined in terms of a measure, and what we could discriminably measure we could then call a role so that quantitatively, too, the types depicted were few and their uniformities, correlates of group process, were stressed accordingly.

Leadership

Perhaps a better contrast may be traced through leadership – a role described and differentiated as no other has been in small-group research and to which its practice has given specific and particular meaning. Traditionally, leadership has been a principle not only about which competing personality theories have made much ado but about which the relevance of personality was rarely questioned. A great variety of doctrines testify to the eminence of its domain, ranging from the heroic to the father-image and from the god-like to the charismatic. All doctrines involved a conviction of the power of the individual to cast his imprint on the course of events so that, by whatever name it was called – genius or extraordinary force or charisma – leadership was identified with personal qualities and the power of personality *vis-à-vis* the group.

In role theory, leadership is first defined in a general way: it is specialized function within the group. In small-group research, however, this definition issued in measures so concrete and specific that leadership became a distinction based

97

upon frequency of interaction or rating scores or sociometric choice. Ordinarily, then, only a doctrine of specificity emerged from these studies: the effective leader was so closely tied to the functions he performed in a particular group that further generalization was difficult. The idea that a leadership principle might emerge to replace the old search for leadership qualities, or that like group conditions would produce emergent leaders of a describable sort, floundered in a deluge of studies using diverse measures and variant criteria. Thus a high interaction rate (Bales), centrality of position (Bavelas), but also distance (Fiedler), and certainly power (Cartwright *et al.*) have all proved significant. Significant also was the reversion to old ideas represented by the attempt to reincorporate 'the great man theory of leadership'. Here the researchers (Borgatta, Couch and Bales, 1955) used combined measures (personality, sociometric) and followed different participants through a number of experimental sessions to arrive at the conclusion that leadership could be identified with the 'generally effective or influential personality'. Thus, far from being inimical, personality and role principles have long mingled in small-group research,* and it depends solely on the researcher whether his design is such as to capture systems effects or personality influences. For most sociological purposes, however, the distinctions pressed are awkward and difficult: leadership is selective, and certain types and traits appear to be bred together, fitting roles – so fitting, in fact, or so suitable to a number of roles that we often speak of 'natural leaders'. Yet such general traits – and they turn up repeatedly as correlations between trait and performance – are meaningless until attached to roles. The attempt to isolate traits that are general for all roles, all groups, or even societies leads us away from those variations in role requirements and role demands that precisely make valuable the

* See, for example, L. Carter, 'Leadership and Small Group Behavior', in M. Sherif and M. Wilson (eds.), *Group Relations at the Crossroads* (1953), for an analysis solely by trait ratings and their factorial sort and for the many endeavours to trace personality effects in the small group setting set forth by W. Haythorn and associates.

possession of some traits and not others. Leadership is universal – it is a role; but its content is variable indeed.

Leadership in the small-group setting led predominantly to redefinition in terms of function and role, but the various criteria of measurement resulted in rather different emphases all the same. Is there, then, an identifiable leadership principle for the small group?

Possibly the most consequential of all findings was Bales's bifurcation of the functional leadership principle into dimensions called instrumental and affective. Seemingly universal group requirements furnished, then, the basis for specialization so that we were indeed given leadership types – two, to be precise. Critics of this strict and narrow operationalism usually point out that, while it has the merit of defining closely what is meant by 'leading', it excludes mixtures and variations and remains remote from real life.

We know what problems and controversies this principle and its perhaps too generous applications have aroused, because, while discovered and measured experimentally, its relevance to real leadership appeared negligible. Its subsequent extensions, however, imperilled any specific political relevance it might conceivably have had. Is the finding too closely tied to the categories and procedures of the coding itself? Is it a by-product of the measuring instrument that required that the data be divided and sorted by its emotional or informational meaning from the very beginning? In any case, ambitious attempts to transfer it to natural small groups like the family (Parsons, Bales *et al.*, 1956) have been strongly contested (Slater, 1961; Levinger, 1964). Its marginal relevance to the analysis of politics and political leadership (Verba, 1961) was long ago pointed up so sharply as to force the whole polemic back into the small world of the small group. There it has remained.

Insistent and rigorous depersonalization of leadership is not notably more conclusive than the personal trait approach of old. Too closely tied to the experimental group, this depersonalization has seemed much too remote and abstract, and its distance from leadership as an essentially 'live' political phenomenon is insuperable. Moreover, different findings – one or another aspect of leadership having been selected for emphasis – have largely served to confirm the irreducibility of leadership to any 'principle'. Thus, an abstract social psychology of leadership – as a group universal for which roles or generalizations could be made – has yielded quite various principles, of power and position, of function and role, of communication and distance; and, therefore, instead of yielding generality, it has yielded specificity.

Alternative approaches to leadership, in the same period as the rise of small-group research, have had other consequences. In a general way, we may say that the social psychology of followership arose as a distinctive psychology of leadership declined, and this change occurred quite independently of role theory. Theories of heroes and great men have been put aside rather than completely dismissed, however; and the imponderables of extraordinary personality have been demeaned, but they have never wholly disappeared. Heroes belong to heroic times and great individuals to periods congenial to individualism. If then, as some have suggested, the idol of our times is the 'collective we', it should be reflected in our social psychology. In the role-set we call 'leader-follower' de-emphasis of the one should cast the other into prominence. Here, a variety of psychologies have played a part; but the most important have built upon individual propensities diffused through whole populations, and the 'personality principle' was then reintroduced as a common psychology applied to collectivities. Hence, individual needs and requirements could be translated into social demands; passivity and fear cry out for authority; willing submission consummates tyranny. This application of personality principles – their collectivization into mass needs expressed through mass movements – is an invention and an insight of modern social psychology that produced a new version of the relation between personality and politics.* No longer was

---

* These are, of course, ideas that formed the core of Fromm's *Fear of Freedom*, and whose parallel in research led to the enormous work of Adorno, Fraenkel-Brunswick *et al.*, *The Authoritarian Personality* (1950).

the analysis of leadership to be the focal point of interest but an analysis of the needs, aspirations and anxieties of followers, which in turn would explain their political choices and political identifications. This very complex proposition, including as it does a host of hypothetical relations between ideology and social psychology as well as personality and politics, constituted the other massive body of research of the period. It is the shift in focus that is of interest here. The authoritarian personality tells us nothing about the structure of political authority from the standpoint of those who lead – only those who follow; little of tyranny – much of the tyrannized; little of coercion – much of compliance; not authority – but dependency. In all of this, we should not see the decline of the 'personality principle' so much as its diffusion and changed expression. In contrast, role theory, with its emphasis on the functions of leadership and role demands, removes personality from the foreground. Personal qualities are not irrelevant; they become significant precisely because they fulfil role demands. Their meaning, therefore, cannot be located in the person as such but in the selection rules and demands of groups and institutions. Small-group research also reflects such rules and demands within the rather narrow limits of its methods and measures (casting forth 'task' and 'emotional' leaders, the bearers of instrumental and affective functions); but in and of itself, such research does not solve the problem of personality. The analysis of leadership should serve to emphasize the fact that in role theory and research it is not the elimination of personality and personal qualities but the resetting of the context and terms of their operation that matters. Nonetheless, to many, here as elsewhere, the role principle has represented the dethronement of personality.

Intimacy

There are other spheres in which sentimental and traditional considerations conflict with the objective analysis of interaction reduced to role taking. Perhaps the most notable of these are spheres of intimacy: here, it has often been claimed, social-structural effects are at minimum; inner needs are given full expression; and formal roles are set aside. This important question is in part exaggerated by the same conditions of modern life that have elevated role analysis to central significance. A by-product of role differentiation itself, the division between private self and public roles comes to appear natural and inevitable. As social roles are accentuated, privacy retained becomes problematic. Are there social relationships that are not dominated by formal requirement and that retain the quality of intimacy?

That the sphere of intimacy was itself bound by rules of interaction, as Georg Simmel (1950, pp. 125–62) emphasized, or that, as small-group researchers have since repeated, typical patterns of interaction can be discerned in friendship, in marriage or in cliques, indicated that these domains of relative singularity and privacy are not immune to role analysis. Private worlds reveal some characteristic differences but rather little pure individuality.

In this sphere, however, personality theorists have busied themselves with the exploration of shared traits and values (value homophyly) or its opposite (complementary trait theories), and with the personality base for attractiveness and attraction. Perhaps the dominant theory to emerge has been one that, instead of a structure of interaction, substitutes for it a theory of psychic structure. Variously known as consistency, balance, or symmetry theories, the patterning discernible in close interaction is referred not to social requisites but to inner psychic strain for order and harmony. Consistency and symmetry here refer to the absence of conflict.

Analysis and research have caused to be put aside once and for all the idea that strictures of size and intimacy might be identifiable with uncomplicatedness and simplicity, or that these might prove prototypic of social process. If the ancient and often repeated belief that individuality (after all, for us equated with the formal freedom that has accompanied the growth of social structures) was best preserved in the small society, or that its morality was superior, or responsibility more certain, analysis of interaction in dyads, triads and other small groups hardly served to support it. The social psychology of intimate interaction accentuates the complexities of social system. Again the choice of adhering closely to an S-R formula or of losing ourselves in the analysis of nuances, of treating interaction as a closed process or introducing into it myriad influences, conditions and circumstances, are all repeated here. For many people, a sociology of intimacy is a contradiction in terms. Should not intimate relationships constitute a test case? Should they not demonstrate the limits of role theory? Should they not be set apart?

Instead interaction analysis invokes the 'reciprocity rule', which tells us that there is a give-and-take principle for these relationships as for most others in life. Worse, this analysis often introduces the language of exchange economics, thereby destroying our fondest hope that somewhere somehow men escape the rule of the market-place.

Friendship as a realm of pure sociability, haven of the ego ideal, or mirror of the alter ego, necessarily bears the burden of excessive idealism and sentiment. Modification of these views has customarily taken two forms.

One form is internal: to subject such relationships to the same kind of interaction analysis as other social roles, relying strongly on notions of role-set, interlocking roles, and above all, the socially limiting conditions within which friendship occurs. Institutional settings (the sociometry of a dormitory for example) or neighbourhoods (Whyte's 'web of friendship' in *Organization Man*, for example) represent the same kind of deromanticization as the ecology of marriage. Friendship, in such a view, is not only conditioned, it is highly predictable. Choice, values and similarity of attitude function within such a narrow range that differences appear trivial. More, the similarities of intimates may subjectively appear as attraction but are likely, objectively, to reflect a set similarity of social background, custom and experience.

Against such upsets to the principles of choice, volition and human affinity stand a number of psychological studies that rely on shared values (value homophyly) or psychic process (balance, symmetry) and sometimes the two in combination (as seen in Newcomb's work). At first glance, it seems as if the rationale of social relationships is not sought within the social situation so much as what is personally delivered to it. Sociometrists often elevated the principle of choice into attraction or personal force or 'tele'. Balance theorists tend to objectify choice as a need for symmetry or harmony; they view choice as a requirement of the smallest social systems. Therefore, what begins as personal attraction ends up as astonishing congruity. The principle of choice is buttressed by values and mutual attraction and sounds personal; it results in closed and harmonious small systems, however, and it is in this fact of balance that is found their *raison d'être*.

Can this be the whole story? If we stand outside these small structures we may well ask other questions about them. Why, for example, do groups differ in a different milieu? Why do some seem to be supported by the environment while others cannot survive at all? Groups may be internally well balanced, and yet their strength and viability depends on more than this fact alone. Sectarian groups, for example, typically display high internal solidarity and value homophyly but their balance is at the mercy of an environment that may or may not permit them to survive. Again, how do we account for the fact of group patterns that give a different 'tone' or 'atmosphere' to towns, cities, regions – all achieving some kind of balance?

Herbert Hyman (in Klineberg and Christie, 1965) has perhaps best stated the limits of attractiveness as a principle when studying small, intimate groups, in showing from his own research that:

. . . there were group situations so defined, so formalized, so normatively structured that individuals were directed toward the ideological features of other people rather than to their profile of personal appeal. The dimensions of popularity were taken out of the realm of chance; they were in the hands of those who created and arranged this special little society [pp. 51–2].

This and his ensuant commentary summarize the kind of criticism that sociologists are likely to bring to preference and friendship studies, i.e. the clear limits to the spontaneously chosen. Those limits are usually indicated by communication networks, ecological arrangements, and the curious fact that the composition of a group happens to be ideally suited to the very kind of group that is wanted, desired, or 'engineered' in a particular milieu. A model of such analysis is Lazarsfeld's and Merton's 'Friendship as a Social Process' (1954). The study was built upon the comparison of friendship choices in two different communities where very different patterns of choice prevailed. In one community a tendency toward choosing status-similar friends was found to be the dominant pattern; in the other community, such was not the case – more open relationships were the rule; status and value-likeness did not coincide. Value homophyly, instead of being taken for granted, was itself a social variable. For these researchers, the whole question of value-likeness was resolved in terms of social setting that made one or the other pattern 'functionally appropriate or inappropriate'.

The analysis of interaction has never been simple and unambiguous, but the apocryphas surrounding the sphere of intimacy require comment. Here, allegedly, is man in, by, and for himself – whether in love, in friendship, or state of familial solicitude. We tend (though it is much too facile) to assume that only in our own time has man been divided against himself. He has long been divided, but the priorities ascribed to public and formal roles as against private and informal ones have differed from time to time. We tend automatically to associate the principle 'to thine own self be true' with the sphere of privacy. Yet we have to draw distinctions here. Withdrawal into privacy is more often an escape device than an assertion of rigorous claim or principle. The pressures of our public roles exert their weight in other ways: the proper marriage, the usefulness of friends, the availability of relatives describe ways in which private relationships expedite or fill out the public and invigorate the self-same private relationships. In so far as roles are not set firm, the person expects to use others and in turn be useful to them. Thus, modern conditions make suspect any accreditation of private roles, as compared to public, in point of genuineness or simplicity, naturalness or noncomplexity, trust or truthfulness. We should, then, quite properly question by what route modern sentiments and sentimentality have come to vest the lasting values of virtue and volition in the sphere of intimacy.

Role theory, viewing man across many roles, can at best hypothesize consistencies or inconsistencies, continuities or discontinuities in the person. We can, in point of fact or logic, name no traits that are reliably associated with private as against public performance. Modern psychological doctrines that have been built on the collapse of privacy and secrecy have dispelled the aura of sanctimony surrounding private life. Hence, we must conclude that whatever aura still surrounds the sphere of privacy lies not in the exercise of virtue but of volition. It remains a retreat – but barely – of choice, of the expression of felt values and needs; at the same time it exaggerates the uniqueness of such needs.

Sociologically, it is almost always assumed that regularities (not necessarily consistencies) between private and public spheres can be demonstrated. Just as private attitudes, opinions and preferences can be located by social group, so too can a variety of behaviours from consumption habits to time budgets, from sexual behaviour to religious belief.* The incursion of the social upon the psychological, and of the determinate upon the volitional, has been so gradual that our changed perspective on these matters is probably measurable only by the disproportionate expression of sentiment toward privacy.

* Sorokin's early *Time Budgets of Human Behavior* (1939) points one way, major consumer studies (tied to advertising) another, the Kinsey report still another. A glance at a reader like R. Bendix's and S. Lipset's *Class, Status and Power* indicates the many directions that 'differential class behaviour' has taken in research and our inclination to stratify group data.

Historically we know that the interplay between private and public roles has varied greatly. The tension between the two that in our own time is occasionally resolved in favour of privacy or *'la vie intérieure'* is but one resolution. Above all, whether the 'authentic' self is sought in private work and private spheres or realized in social tasks has not always been a viable alternative. The ancient Stoic saw things rather differently: to 'submit to the dictates of reason' in sacrifice 'for the good of the city-state' could mean freedom from the mere 'bonds of human affection' or mere selfhood.

The priorities emphasized or choices demarcated indicate our own definitions of self, role, and character. The conception of character itself has been driven further and further inward. Long before modern psychologies ascribed depth and genuineness to what was hidden from view, we had learned to endow intimacy with genuineness and sincerity and left the public self as mere mask. Role theory reflects these antinomies, too, but seeks a different resolution. This resolution involves no clear cleavage between selves but an investigation of man in his multiplicity; no begging of the question of essential differences between intimate and formal roles but a search for the rules that govern each or both; no dream that freedom and autonomy, deep within the self, are expressively released just in those relations we call friendly or intimate. Ultimately, of course, role theory has meant externalizing the character of man and stressing its demystification.

Character Analysis and Role Analysis

The analytic and interpretative influence of role theory has derived from a changed social world and changed social relations. The areas of great change – those marked by confused definitions or conflicting choice – are areas in which the relevance of character and personality have been debated most keenly. Examples are: sex roles (the feminine character), nation (the national character), politics (the authoritarian personality), and crime (the delinquent personality). In each of these instances (and each represents large areas of research), the problem of personality has been debated repeatedly and, in each, competing role theories have upset fixed characterologies.

THE FEMININE CHARACTER

This popular controversy rests upon the most elementary and universal differentiation known: everywhere given biological differences between men and women are accompanied by differences in occupation, social codes, and rules of behaviour; everywhere a basic categorical difference between sexes is given; everywhere there are differences, but no consistent differences. Thus, the principle of the 'eternal feminine', which role analysis in methodic and pedestrian fashion denies, presents problems of mythic rather than mundane importance: as a universal category of difference there has been gathered about it an elaborate symbolization of all contrasts (in nature, in social life, in religion), and at the same time it comes to represent a first and final principle of difference itself.

Here, altogether more prosaic concerns have animated the debate: feminine 'roles' or the feminine 'character' – a sociology of sex or a biopsychology? The one emphasizes variance, the other uniformity; the one sees change, the other changelessness. In the face of numerous, complex and diverse definitions of the feminine role, the first approach claims there are no rules we can draw from the lessons of biology. In the name of the same biology, the other approach sees a certain bondage if not in household, at least in hormones. Generally, the more relative femininity is shown to be (in work allocation, in childbirth customs, in legal status), the sharper the counter-emphasis on discrete biological factors. General physical inferiority or weakness or passivity, for example, have given way to rather more obscure doctrines of the biopsychology of sex differences. Biology is still the beginning and end of all characterologic doctrines, however, from instinct theories to psychoanalysis. Old evolutionary theories alternated between a view of the battle of the sexes as a relation between conqueror and conquered that would explain widespread enslavement and subordination – or its opposite, original insubordination (the matriachate) followed by usurpation of power. These old theories are one indication why other generations focused on power differentials (legal and political emancipation were key issues) where we see only sex differences. The feminine character has narrowed to mere biology, its former accompanying traits disappearing into comparative role analysis.

Yet that character has been redefined so often and persistently that it has, appropriately, been ascribed the weight of ideology (Klein, 1949). It is an ideology designed to explain power and status differences, and it is a label we can use only because those differences have long been challenged not just by social and political movements but by the fact of social change itself. Role shifts and the redefinition of roles engender conflict, but conflict itself is a category whose psychological status has risen as the older psychology of women has declined. We may take it to signal the relocation of feminine psychology from the sphere of bio- to sociopsychology, and this shift is understandable only in the light of role analysis.

It is significant that 'conflict' was not a current term at the time when women suffragettes marched in the streets in militant demonstrations for civil rights. Instead, it is allegedly a characteristic feature of contemporary women, a legacy of 'emancipation', so it is said, and a diffused and vague discomfort following upon many possible choices and many possible roles. Such discomfort leads to that chronic dissatisfaction that, like the hysteria of a bygone time, is a recognizably feminine malaise.

But the conversion of role analysis to psychological slogan – from objective social situation to subjective unhappiness – is, at best, misleading. And here, as there is no feminine role without role-set, interaction theory requires us to observe that if there is feminine role conflict, there is almost inevitably masculine role conflict too. Therewith we comfront some very old issues.

Women represent the only minority group that is not a

true minority. They share the same immutable experience of negative rank bound to ascriptive criteria. That this can be transcended individually (extraordinary achievement) or psychologically (exploiting pure femininity) hardly matters – the same possibilities typify most minorities. As groups, in many of their social roles and accompanying social psychology, we can see a host of parallels. Sex, like ethnicity or age, is a basic social category, familiarly referred to as ascriptive status, which also carries rank. There is a tendency to draw a too sharp and perhaps facile line between ascribed and achieved status according to the possibilities of change we call mobility, for it suggests that ascriptive status is fixed and unchangeable and that achieved status is not.* But a rank order cuts across both; the social position of the whole group can be as eventually changed as an individual life through changes in rank, but the way in which change occurs is totally different.

When we speak of social mobility we mean individual movement into another stratum (class); we have no corresponding term to account for changes in the ascriptive status of whole groups. Sometimes they have been called revolutions, the greatest of which we view as finished (i.e. they successfully consummated change); the lesser ones are notably unfinished and therefore remain social problems. We view as finished the great revolutions that destroyed the old aristocratic order (France, Russia) and re-established governments 'of, by and for' the people. We may view as unfinished the feminist revolution that ended with enfranchisement but left a recognizable 'woman problem'.

* Such confusion is perpetuated by a rigorous 'systematic' sociology whose proponents alternate between a search for cultural universals and a doctrinaire insistence on tidy distinctions – no longer between stages of social evolution, but between types of societies. Not only are certain categories of ascriptive status universal but certain societies are ruled by an ascriptive order as against modern societies whose rule of achievement demolishes the ascriptive order. Sometimes, in eagerness to establish the universality of ascription, rank was set aside: but to establish the validity of the traditional, the remarkable coalescence of the two was emphasized (as in caste).

The old feminists by no means limited their concern to the political and economic problems of women. It was clear enough to them that what was required was emancipation from their sexual role. When sexual emancipation arrived, however, far from freeing women, it preached the fulfilment that comes with bondage. This, in its contemporary form, we know as feminine psychology. Some writers have gone so far as to maintain that the sexual revolution (in effect, no revolution) was itself instrumental in killing feminism. The sexual revolution is clearly incomplete, however, and a combination of effective birth-control programmes and population policy may ultimately complete it without reference to either feminism or feminine psychology. The sexual fulfilment of women in childbearing has in the past accorded remarkably well with various social norms of desirable family size: the big prosperous Victorian family as against the middle-sized, middle-income, middle-class family, for example, or the big rural family as against the small city one. If the population theorists are right, abundance, abundant sexual fulfilment and feminine emancipation can be simultaneously achieved by voting for childlessness.

Meanwhile, changes in the position of women have been multifarious, but they may also prove to be transitory. These changes leave unresolved issues and problems that may be regarded as an unfinished revolution or no revolution at all. Like age groups or minority groups, the position of women changes with 'macroscopic' changes in the social field; such we measure as trends to which the question of final significance or outcome is really quite irrelevant, and surely not discernible. War influences the occupational structure of women; tax laws may shift the distribution of wealth and property to women; population policy may facilitate, or reverse, the movement of women in and out of jobs; new technologies may, by another combination of circumstance, favour women (laboratory technicians, computer technicians).

Many of the 'revolutionary' changes are of this cumulative, indirect, and cross-cutting sort: they are structural effects of change in complex societies, change that bears differently on different groups. Since they are neither self-propelled nor ever wholly independent of the position of other groups or the working of other factors, the position (roles) of women is complex but not uniquely so – and much the same might be said for all accompanying conflicts. If we narrow our terms to traditional political meanings we might well contend that a decisive reversal of former conditions obtained but still set the emancipation of women in the context of the great reform movements of enfranchisement. Nonetheless, sex role is a variable we have to reckon with whether we are dealing with vital statistics or occupational distributions, religious or political behaviours, crime or psychopathology. Were we to take as our criterion the absence of such differences, we should have to say that evidence for an egalitarian revolution is lacking. This lack, however, suggests neither a permanency of feminine character nor under-emphasis of marked changes in roles. Moreover, the position of women – their ascribed rank upward or downward in different societies – is a highly significant indicator and an overall evaluation that can be described and measured through specifying comparative roles and functions.

While feminine roles are everywhere differentiated from masculine ones, they are by no means uniform across cultures. Thus, we distinguish the advantages women usually possess in matrilineal as compared to patrilineal societies regarding clan support, rights over children, freedom of separation and divorce. Moreover, we cannot equate feminine roles in ancient Greece or Rome with those of the Middle Ages or pioneer America. Yet summary discussions of the feminine role are quite common and even appear valid if we detach role analysis from the working of institutions. This detachment permits universalizing the role as such or its presumed psychic accompaniments, or both. The most conspicuous instance of universalizing is to circumscribe the feminine role about the maternal role, or to read as culturally universal the 'affective' functions of women as against the 'instrumental' functions of men (Parsons, Bales *et al.*, 1956). Role analysis has accommodated to other archaic feminine-masculine themes in substituting for objective role analysis a host of subjective role responses, most notable of which has been that of role conflict. Where objective role conflict exists, however, we have, it may be observed, a social problem, not a psychological one (of working mothers or parentless children, for example); and where psychic conflicts over choice are at issue, it is rare that role conflict suffices to explain the irresolution. The complex relation of women to occupational opportunity has not been clearly advanced by a role psychology that construes this relation in terms of private choice and conflict. It is rather like explaining the sexual distribution of occupations in terms of voluntary role restriction.

It is in the occupational sphere that feminism, the sexual revolution, minority problems, and class factors come to converge. First, since the Industrial Revolution, the domestic emancipation of women has meant different things depending upon social class. Emancipation for one group meant the wage slavery of factory labour, for another the choice of independence through professional services (some of which were open and some closed to women), for yet others a conventional passage from the domicile of origin to that acquired by marriage.

It is as little appropriate to speak of the emancipation of women in relation to the second Industrial Revolution as it is to the first (Baker, 1965). The new careers, the office and professional services that are virtually identified as women's work, indicate the formidable weight of sexual status. The apparent mobility of women, in this respect, is comparable to the intergenerational data on class mobility: much of it must be attributed to external occupational shifts and changed opportunities. Overall, the change was good but represented no dramatic advancement. Above all, it indicated that women might avail themselves of such opportunities as were presented but did not, apparently, go out of their way to seize them. Their alleged passivity is presumed to supply the psychological link to other minorities whose position may also rise or fall according to available opportunities but whose very concentration in certain occupations suggests an absence of choice.

Second, ethnic and sex variables that objectively look something alike in their workings may be seen as absolutely different once social class is introduced as an intervening factor. Sexual rank (unlike ethnic) cuts across all social classes so that we cannot speak of a 'common fate' of women but instead must stratify their occupations and ways of life according to class position. Once political rights were won, there remained few common issues that could unite women; but basic legal definitions and rights are central to the new liberation groups.

Finally, their occupational roles will continue to involve a host of traditional issues. Further emancipation from familial roles does not necessarily mean that the economy provides alternate occupations. Nor does it suggest that such occupations as are provided will improve women's status. The increments have been small; there is little to suggest that they will be greatly enlarged in the future. Instead, increasing specialization may well reinforce existing patterns of 'women's work' and 'men's work'. Such role congruities can become highly conventionalized even if domesticity declines.

We have suggested above that many of the new terms of role analysis have often done service for the feminine character. Emphasis on strict sex role differences regularly has this consequence as if sociologists themselves had forgotten John Stuart Mill's old observation about the position of women that 'everything which is usual appears natural'. Role analysis in no sense implies a negation of sex differences; it does imply that everything that is usual is so conventionalized that we can no longer distinguish what is natural. Far from giving us cultural universals, it suggests attentiveness to the social setting of sexual roles. The same is true of the stylization of women at different times, in different places, and by social stratum. We should hardly be able to understand the lady and the whore, the factory girl and the débutante, the careerist or the sportswoman, if we see in each not feminine role differentiation but simply the feminine role.

A similar caution should prevail when we are dealing with cultures other than our own. It may, for example, come to us as a surprise to learn of India that:

> The history of the early Indian period reads like that of a perfectly modern and individualistic society. . . . Women had the same freedom and equality as men; there was absolutely no seclusion. Women sometimes had more education than men and had a prominent position in religious and social gatherings. Monogamy was the rule. . . . In India boys and girls underwent a ceremony of *upanayana* or initiation into education together. . . . It is well known that women were among the great Upanisadic philosophers . . . [S. K. Saksena (1968), p. 348].

THE NATIONAL CHARACTER

Like feminine character, the idea of national character appears all but immortal. Whether we believe that we are seeing the sunset of old nationalism or the sunrise of a new, national character as a unifying symbol lingers on as sentiment, as quasi-racial legend, as communication theory (the linguistic community), as statistical norm (modal personality), and as historical memory (the historical community). Its anachronistic aspect has long been evident in analyses of international relations that depend on power and balance of power concepts, or on interaction models of games and strategy and coalition formation, to none of which the idea of character is useful. Nonetheless, national character has appeared wonderfully adaptive to shifting power positions, its uses legion. Reischauer (1965) once described the case of Japan this way:

> Little Japan's military victory in 1894 and 1895 over China, the monster sleeping dragon of Asia, was greeted with the plaudits of the entire Western world. During her uphill fight against Russia, the colossus of the north, Japan had no more sympathetic friend than President Theodore Roosevelt . . . and there was no small degree of friendship in his action in engineering a peace treaty in 1905 at Portsmouth. . . . But the Russo-Japanese war marked both the high water mark of Japanese-American friendship and a sharp turning point. . . .

115

Japan and America now stood alone in the Pacific. . . . The charmingly quaint and admirably quick Japanese had suddenly become for us the sinister Yellow Peril.

Recent theories of national character – long since dethroned from prominence in history and politics – became social psychology (sometimes 'psychological anthropology') and as such went to war and survived the peace.* This in itself is unusual: roused by war, the old national character theorists were lulled by peace.

Dispassionately, we have long known concern with national character as the study of stereotypes and stereotypy – that is, the social-psychological exploration of categorization, circularity, and fixed errors in perception and cognition. For all practical purposes, in social psychology stereotype and character remain indistinguishable. And since groups are, like individuals, ascribed a 'character', an 'ethos', or 'traits', the question becomes: In what terms should they be cast for research and interpretation? Should we detach ourselves from the task of error-free characterization or should we grasp its analytic possibilities? Should we recognize the 'sidedness' of our socially rooted judgements and perceptions and opt for straightforward attitude and opinion studies or press for the appraisals of a competent study of character? There is a vast difference between using character ascriptions as data – i.e. as a criterion, a measure, a social index – and searching for valid characterizations to summarize the social psychology of whole groups. The one task is limited, provisional and essentially sceptical; the other is ambitious, arbitrary, and faithful to a theory, if not a science, of character.

The investigation of stereotypes – essentially research into the creation, perpetuation and change of attitudes toward

* Reference is to the multitude of studies during the Second World War and immediately after, centring on Germany, Japan and Russia. Examples are: H. V. Dicks, 'German Personality Traits and National Socialist Ideology' (1950), pp. 111–54; G. Gorer and J. Rickman, *People of Great Russia* (1949); J. Maloney, *Understanding the Japanese Mind* (New York, Philosophical Library, 1954); and M. Mead, *Soviet Attitudes Toward Authority* (1951).

other groups – acquired international scope following its exploration on the American scene. Highly repetitive and limited in its procedures, it has by now spread around the world to the newest nations as well as the oldest. Recent attempts to revivify it on an ambitious scale (Campbell and LaVine, 1961) – i.e. to assemble as many cultural samples as possible of its workings – use the stereotypy concept as a kind of universal social-psychological mechanism and depart emphatically from the old categories of perception that guided the early investigations of stereotypes.

But it is in the post-war surveys of international attitudes (sponsored by UNESCO) that the largest efforts lay; and we may attend to them momentarily, for they encompass a major shift in attitude toward attitude studies. There was once a dream – the major impetus for the original studies – that, having demonstrated stereotyped prejudices, we might rise above them and that education in tolerance and understanding would set things right in the world. But instead the extended study of stereotypy bred a certain cynicism and futility, the gentlest résumé of which was made by Buchanan and Cantril in their UNESCO survey (1953). There the relation between public stereotypes and public policy, attitudes and international politics was summarized this way: 'The tenor of findings as a whole is in the direction of minimizing the causative effect of either favourable or unfavourable stereotypes in relations between nations, and suggests that stereotypes may not exist until objective events demand their creation' (p. 57). Studies of change in stereotypes during the war (Meenes, 1947) were rather undramatic compared to the very rapid realignments following the war, the ones that Buchanan and Cantril studied. Meanwhile, the domestic scene on which the original stereotypy studies had grown was changing rapidly. There was, first, the much-heralded decline in stereotypy (Gilbert, 1951; Bettelheim and Janowitz, 1964) and beyond that, on all sides, indications of an important reversal regarding the uses of the concept.

It is apparent that as long as stereotypy was regarded as a fixed perceptual distortion that could be corrected only by

117

education and enlightenment, change would be slow and gradual; but new movements the world over challenged inaction. Formally and academically the changeability of stereotypes had been explored, and stereotypes came to be regarded as a standard adjunct of intergroup relations and an aspect of group ideology or group policy. It was a new social movement that challenged both fixity and inaction, however, and in its wake not the validity but the relevance of stereotypes paled. Thus 'new nationals' everywhere (including the Negro rights movement in the United States) regarded stereotypy with the same disdain that feminists had regarded the traditional feminine character.

In contrast, national character types have been constructed by drawing upon different psychological or social traits and the resultant 'type' subsequently used to summarize uniformities or to predict the behaviours of other national groups. If we glance at the traits studied, however, we see at once the meeting ground of character and stereotype: not the perceptual content but only the terms in which each is presented vary. The traits the character analyst reworks are the same traits of popular national character depiction whether we assemble them from adjectives used in newspapers and periodicals or from checklists submitted to students. As with the standard content of stereotypes, we have to ask: If the picture is neither true nor false but a way of seeing others, how useful can we judge it to be and how shall we judge its uses?

Typically the passions of war and the sweet reason of peace have led to quite different judgements. We should do well to remember here Morris Ginsberg's apt phrase in characterizing all national character literature as *'livres de circonstance'*.

While notional character types were allegedly built as 'psychological types', procedures used to arrive at their definition have been various, unsystematic, and poorly controlled. Literary sources were typically drawn upon; putative but unconfirmed child-training patterns (Gorer on the Japanese, Margaret Mead and Gorer and Rickman on Russia) or family structure (Dicks on Germany) were typical points of approach to the character analysis of whole nations. While Freudian typologies have been the most obvious source for the characterology, diagnostic psychological tests have occasionally been used, and particular traits (anxiety, dominance, competitiveness) in turn were used as the core about which a character was constructed. Such was the procedure Kluckhohn and his associates used in comparing a sample of Russian refugees with a sample of Americans (in Inkeles and Geiger, 1961). Neither procedure can be easily justified as a basis for projecting national character, though the problem is hardly one of sampling alone. An array of wholly theoretical difficulties centres quite separately on the question of the uses and misuses of psychoanalytic theory (Hartmann, Kris, and Lowenstein, 1951) in the one case, and on the *ad hoc* creation of character out of disparate test-traits in the other.

The last difficulty is perhaps the most obvious and conspicuous criticism of proposals for the strictly empirical redefinition of national character as a statistical artifact called 'modal personality' (Inkeles and Levinson, 1969). It would presumably present trait distributions but not types. Yet it must also be remarked about this approach (as of the measurement of national character quite generally) that while everyone likes to talk about it, the joyous labour of demonstrating the disparate distribution of all too human characteristics has drawn few enthusiasts.

Even the most empirical of character descriptions requires a theory of character in terms of which traits are made meaningful. If such a theory is not set forth at the outset, it is made manifest in the uses to which fresh character data are put. Thus, the character uncovered in Kluckhohn's Russian refugee sample was arbitrarily designated the traditional character of Russians; it was sharply contrasted with the character of the new Soviet man – untested, but constructed from official Bolshevik ideology. Between the traditional and the new, the researchers felt they had possibly come upon a national character drama. If so, its fateful consequences have never been revealed, and the implied relationship of character to political belief or political action remains obscure.

The search for and the uses to which the new character types have been put have always been accompanied by noisy acclamation and declamation. The imperfection of their methods and procedures is less grave, as many see it, than the uses and purposes they have directly and sometimes mischievously served. Are there clear lines along which an impartial and dispassionate research can be pursued?

In determining and measuring differences between groups, reasons of economy alone might be adduced for avoiding the idea of character. Survey research routinely measures different attitudes and opinions and, it has often been argued, keeps reasonably clear what we can and cannot do (Smith, 1966). But the fair testing of a fair sample of the populations of modern nations is unlikely to yield clear types or even clusters of traits. It is a lucky researcher who even hits upon an occasional trait markedly over-represented in one national sample when compared to another. Thus Farber's old comparative study of British and American insurance clerks hit upon apparently significant differences in response to one question on his schedule, where 'go-getting' qualities were mentioned in 31 per cent of the American responses but in only 7 per cent of the English, while ability to control impulses was given in 30 per cent of the English responses and in only 8 per cent of the American (cited in G. Allport, 1954). McGranahan (1946) found a few differences comparing samples of American high-school students and German boys. Among the differences regarded as significant was the following: to the question which of two boys is worse, one who disobeys his superiors or one who bullies and beats up smaller children, 68 per cent of the Americans specified the latter while only 41 per cent of the Germans did. More recently, Milgram (1961), using a familiar type of conformity experiment, compared Norwegian and French students. In all of the tests the French revealed larger percentages of independent judgements, but the differences were not great.

Both groups showed similar tendencies toward independence under conditions of privacy and discretion (written rather than vocal responses); both displayed greater conformity under pressure.

It is evident that such comfort as we find in these researches derives not from the compellingness of the data but from their closeness to older stereotypes and character conceptions. Impracticality and paucity of findings have rather successfully deterred extension of painstaking, systematic research into national character.

But against these problems we must place the inextinguishable fascination of the idea of character that in times of crisis, like any other reservoir of folk wisdom, is searched for signs and portents to guide the affairs of men. If we ask what is the purpose of whole characterization and how important it is to unveil the ethos of a society, we would have to aver that its symbolic importance is enormous and its practical value nil. Nowhere is this more evident than in those artful constructions of the past that worked with a very different view of character and culture and yet have left us with general procedures for relating the two.

In that old view character was not at all to be equated with psychological character but referred to style, forms of expression, cultural patterns and configurations. We know that in the recent equations of character and culture a conspicuous difficulty lay in the imperfections of the analogy: character was to biography as culture was to history; but in transposing psychological categories, it was not the vicissitudes of the particular nation or the nation's history that were used but the typical vicissitudes of its members. In isolating national traits, explanation was sought at an individual psychological level so that, in effect, every national was regarded as a microcosm of his nation. And the newness of the idea of social character or basic personality could simply be written off as an undemonstrated and probably undemonstrable summary statement of individual character within given national boundaries.

In contrast, ambitions of characterizing whole cultures have

evolved independently of characterology but have stayed close
to history; there the aim was not to discover the psychologically shared but to emphasize the historically distinctive. As far as national character itself was concerned, interest
was never in national virtue but in virtuosity, that is to say,
in uniqueness and genius. It was not the common character
of man that was regarded as crucial but the uncommon,
extraordinary character of the few. These were the true
bearers of culture and history, so it was said, and they have
travelled under various names as representative men, culture
heroes, and élites. Representing an old aristocratic theory of
culture and character, we know the theory and all its col-
laterals well, simply as élitism.

The complexities of modern societies and politics have
engendered scant enthusiasm for the search for ethos, but in
modern pluralist conceptions, the differentiation of social
strata is of commanding importance. The role of the leading
strata, the circulation of élites, the diffusion or democratiza-
tion of dominant types become separate and separable problems and lead into the definition of character in terms of
social roles – though they are decidedly not psychological
types. Similarly, institutional congruities, symmetry within
organized social life, cultural pattern or configuration have
all represented special developments of the exploration of
societies or epochs in terms of style, and many have involved
individual historical types regarded as exemplary bearers of
that style (Renaissance man, feudal knight, Japanese samurai).
But all refer to and are defined in terms of social roles, not
psychological character.

We can perhaps best summarize the limits of role versus
character principle by a cursory review of terms in the
analysis of international relations. There was once a traditional, familistic view of the nations of Europe – its great-
power and small-power nations dwelling together – which
collapsed with the First World War. This cosy view of the
'family of nations' became a historic point of reference not
because it ever existed but because it had animated the
dreams of pacifists and internationalists and at the same time

incorporated the only noble aspects to be derived from the literature of nationalism – namely, the essential democracy and equipotentiality of all nations.

National character and national culture together constituted the genius of a people, which could be viewed as represented by the few élite theory) or the many (democratic theory). So long as an international order could be conceived as ordered, roles could be set and nations might be thought to possess a stable and durable national character.

Into this comity of nations broke the realities of power politics: entangling treaties and alliances, the scramble for markets, the aggrandizements of the 'upstart' nations. Efforts to interpret international anarchy shifted to the analysis of power and position, of move and counter-move, of coalitions and alliances, of games and strategies; and such is the case today. In the interim – in the recrudescence of national character theories in the war and immediate post-war period – the fixed positions of the great powers could plausibly appear as characterology, and national character disquisitions could simply be read as part of national ideology. Still, official policy, ideology, and character could appear of a piece only so long as there were no 'third worlds' to disturb these closed systems. New events accentuate but do not alter the fact that for the game of politics the moral, aesthetic or psychological requirements of character analysis belong to another world.

THE AUTHORITARIAN PERSONALITY

All character analysis is predicated on the proposition that character is sufficiently consistent to formulate rules between character and behaviour – hence the minimizing of all situational factors that induce uniformities of behaviour and hence disinterest in interaction analysis that uncovers regularities in terms of an S-R formula, ongoing actions and reactions of participants, or alignment and realignment of positions in social space.

But the basic presupposition of all personality theory, that consistency and unity of person leads to consistent and predictable behaviours, has remained an article of faith precisely because it is almost impossible to demonstrate. The discrepancy between our experience of person and our ability to formulate that experience scientifically has led to a curious and fixed division between theory and practice, between what personality theorists talk about and what they do. In theory, the conviction of personal unity, coherence, and consistency is maintained; in practice, the search for a proper key to its analysis has led to a bewildering variety of tests and measures. Almost invariably the use of one or another such key evokes a torrent of controversy, for generally there emerges a fragile structure built upon altogether too fragile foundations. In social psychology the most important keys have centred on clues to the analysis of social behaviour through the common possession of particular individual traits. This approach, of course, destroys the essential meaning of personality and at the same time confounds our interpretations and may, therefore, account for the wide areas of dispute. We can see that the problem is identical to the one the researcher hits upon when he selects a group according to 'trait'. The trait becomes standardized (or conventionalized) and can no longer discriminate for us. It becomes a social trait not a personal one. Contrarily, if it is truly personal, its uses as a social instrument are limited.

Resurrection of the search for predictable relationships between a personality syndrome and social-political attitudes was dramatically embodied in the definitions of the authoritarian personality. The ambitiousness of the original research, the voluminous research engendered in its name, and its power of argument were all achieved. If political convictions really lay so close to the heart of man, if they were truly consistent and of a piece, or if the association of traits and beliefs were as intimate as the research suggested then a major discovery would indeed have been made. Instead the research constituted a major dispute. We can only conclude that its theory of the patterning of early traits (compensatory over-identification with authority and the displacement of hostility from parents who are loved and feared to social objects who are not loved but feared) may give us the key to the authoritarian personality in life, in politics, and in social relations but no general key to politics, prejudice or social relations.

The authoritarian personality is the last major monument we have to trait measurement, and much dispute went into item analysis, the phenomenon of acquiescent response, and subsequent test revision. Yet today, while perhaps no one doubts that the authoritarian personality does exist, no one takes this fact as a guide to the phenomenon of prejudice and even less to the complexities of politics. Its uses have shrunk to the negligible and its application narrowed to the routine use of the F-scale as another personality test.

From the sociological standpoint, the basic difficulty was an old one. How can we distinguish personal from social traits – bigotry from conventional prejudice, violent discrimination from passive antagonism – if all alike are because of personality? Or, stated from the direction of society: How can we explain the appearances and disappearances of prejudice, its uneven expression, its cultural regions and its history, if all lies within the person? The sociologist typically refers to the age, regional, class and educational differences that undo the pure working of the personality principle as it was hypothesized in the original research. Thus, prejudice in children increases with age and grade in school; in the United States, Southern samples test differently from Northern, giving only moderate correlations between anti-Semitic and anti-Negro attitudes; lower-class samples have regularly showed higher (F-scale) authoritarian scores; so have less educated ones. Cultural regions of high prejudice do not yield commensurate measures of authoritarianism (Yinger and Simpson, 1958; Pettigrew, 1958).

The sociological circumstances have changed too. Like the stereotypy research that preceded it, the practical implications of the authoritarian personality scarcely fit the current scene. The covert preachment of the one was neutrality, detachment, and education; of the other, personality change and psychotherapy. The psychopathology of prejudice, like education in tolerance and enlightenment, does not bear well under the onslaught of an activist politics of civil rights and may even present itself as delaying and obstructionist doctrine. Even modest social change, in the interim, has suggested more practical possibilities. Hence, the living situation – whether of mixed crews and platoons and schools (desegregation studies), or of neighbourhoods and housing projects – has also given important data for changing interaction patterns. As hope and interest in social experiments rose, interest in fixed conceptions of personality declined.

The immediate social and political context within which such researches have been pursued is so intimately bound to them that their specific propositions get lost and forgotten. Here, the character hypothesis – with its search for a regular relationship between personality and political choice – has been set aside as unproved and probably unprovable, and more reliable and expedient guides to political choice emerge from the bare sociological data of region, class, education or ethnic group.

THE DELINQUENT PERSONALITY

It is always instructive to trace changing perspectives and interpretations of cherished theories of the past, not in order to dismiss them but to prepare us for their restatement. Whether it is a question of the movement of women from traditional to new roles, challenging an old fixity of character and social positions; of shifting international positions that make of national character a misconceived emphasis in the interpretation of world politics; of a civil rights movement that clamoured for the righting of wrongs irrespective of a fixity or stereotype or psychopathology of attitude; or, finally, of social change sufficiently complex to make clear differentiation of criminal and noncriminal a problem in itself; in all of these instances the statement and restatement of problems in social psychology have been intimately bound to the 'real world'. We understand the feminine character of the Victorian world in the same way that we understand the authoritarian personality in an era of authoritarianism.

Of all these comparisons, the 'criminal character', nowadays called the 'delinquent personality', is likely to us to seem the most anachronistic and the most improbable of all propositions put forth in the name of psychological theory. That psychopathic criminality occurs is beyond question; that a variety of character disorders may, but does not necessarily, lead to crime is also clear. Would controlled psychological testing of 'criminal' and 'normal' populations establish clinical differences between the two? Sociologists generally doubt it. Demonstrating psychological peculiarities constituent of criminality is not just a difficult task; its futility is usually spelled out by observing that as long as the definition of crime and the criminal vary by time and place and circumstance, the definition of criminal personality is impossible. Nonetheless, criminal types used to abound. What has happened to them? Will they return?

Chronic disjointedness of the times points to the inadequacy of all formerly favoured theories. Old sociological doctrines that explained crime as the social cost of social problem groups (relying heavily on delinquency rates and delinquency areas) are all but *passés*. The facts are there but our interpretation of them has changed considerably. This change is similarly true of the newer doctrines relating crime or delinquency to the 'opportunity structure'. Neither the 'social problem' theory of yesterday nor that of the 'opportunity structure' today serves to interpret middle-class criminality or the new suburban crime rates. Each disguises the fact that a new social psychology of crime is substituting for the old criminology. Ever since Sutherland discovered 'white-collar crime', there has been reluctant acknowledgment that crimes of force and fraud bear differential relation to type of social structure. But our explorations of wrongdoing remain remarkably limited.

It may be observed that in the language of deviation, all current theoretical quandaries are set adrift. The deviant has replaced the criminal character and delinquent personality of yesterday; he is wayward in strictly statistical terms, permitting us to take cognizance of changing norms. But he can also

127

be defined in role terms ('outsider'), or formal structural terms (nonconformity to institutional requirements). What is called deviant includes all categories traditionally included in criminal codes (con man, hobo, addict, embezzler, tax dodger, and the usual felonies). Technically, 'deviant' sounds less morally censorious and has the advantage of seeming neutrality. It is also a way of incorporating the language of role into the old criminology, and it is a way of substituting for the delinquent personality a behavioural definition of the criminal.

Roles and Traits

In all of these comparisons it might well be said that the language of role has simply (and often superficially) supplanted the language of character analysis, that the abstract analysis of a role may differ little from that of abstract character, and that, after all, sociologists work with 'types' too, so that our distinctions remain unclear.

An important reason why they remain unclear is the common confusion of psychological with social types and our inability to force their separation. Psychological types appear as universalizations of some aspect of man that is socially shaped and therefore overdetermined despite the appearance of being naturally given. For the sociologist it is always what is given but variously shaped that is of first interest. If we run through the common foundations for a character of man, we would simply recite the evolution of characterologies based on instinct, then on temperament, then constitutional theories followed by those of psychosexual stages and a variety of value orientations. All now furnish us a base for a tedious exercise in cross-cultural noncomparability. Abstracted from time and place and circumstance, all were assumed to be common human propensities; but just as in origin they were built upon local and particular observations, so too their applicability is limited to local and particular uses. Thus we are left in our own cultural arena with testing correlations between our own psychological types and a multitude of interesting variables from race to politics, from social class to sex, from crime to physical and psycho-pathology.

But our variables are notoriously impure, and in social and social-psychological research this impurity (or overlap) is repeatedly demonstrated by our ability to design research in which we can interchange our definitions of dependent and independent variable and almost unfailingly emerge with meaningful results. Instances abound.

We can find the authoritarian character in an authoritarian milieu – or we can reverse the proposition and compare milieus to prove the inconsistency of character; we can find the achievement motive behind every achieving society or we can show that the conditions of society set the motives for achievement; we can aver that leaders possess the trait of dominance or we can prove that dominance accompanies position or task or office.

The very social rootedness of our psychological types suggests why we can never wholly isolate them from social types and social roles; yet our way of measuring types (sociological and psychological) – trait by trait analysis usually – yields poor correlations. Why this is so seems transparently simple: traits detached from their social expression (roles) have no validity and no meaning. We pick them up as correlations when they are allied to roles (the piety of the cleric, the introversion of the scholar, the ascendancy of the leader); we lose them when they are not. The person carries – he does not create – traits, and their appearance, their strength and their meaning derive from roles he has played and roles he learns. On occasion this has been experimentally demonstrated by placing subjects who test high or low on ascendancy measures in a central position in a group and comparing their performance. Those who test high perform smoothly from the beginning, but after a few trials the initial differences disappear and the two types tend to become alike (Berkowitz, 1956). But the emergence of traits from roles learned and performed in no way simplifies personality; it does make the sources of personality more complex than traditional personality theories allow. Traditionally, traits are treated as independent variables; as personal behaviours they correlate with role performance because, presumably, all those who fill a particular role possess the trait in question. The fact that we sometimes find traits and role requirements to be highly correlated, however, does not prove the independence of either one. The dominance of the leader, the submissiveness of the servant, and the punctuality of the clerk are examples of traits so well correlated with role that we can define them as role requirements. None of them furnishes a good case of proof or disproof to a favoured theory, be it personality or role. The irrelevance of many personality traits derives from a different source; it comes from our inability to prove their relation to role performance. If traits do not dovetail with role requirement, we often have to assume that they are neutral or adaptive to different organizational requirements. Anxiety, rigidity, introversion and extraversion are psychic traits that are worked out in various ways in different social contests. When we try to fit them to particular groups – political, occupational, religious, the delinquent, the young – the fit is a poor one. From the beginning we have to be much more specific in defining the possible relation of trait to role performance; usually role analysis provides us a handy reference to what is selectively permitted or approved, sanctioned or required.

Social groups do indeed breed types, but no one yet has successfully fitted them to psychological types. The selection of traits – and sometimes conspicuous selection – presents us with no psychological syndromes. Yet there remain numerous social types, without which neither history nor anthropology nor sociology could do at all. Generally, we do best if we simply and decisively differentiate these categories from all psychological types. Grave and wicked disputes may be engendered merely by calling Weber's Puritan of the Protestant Ethic an anal neurotic or by attempting to decide whether, for example, the bureaucrat is introverted, as Merton's bureaucratic personality would seem to suggest, or extroverted like Whyte's organization man.

In social life our task is one of role description, and here we should stress that types are defined not in terms of psychic traits (he who wishes to measure these may do so) but in terms of social behaviour and social location. They are always individual-historical types. Often we identify type by epoch (Renaissance man, Puritan colonist) or epoch by man (organization man, feudal knight), but there is no role-type without specific social location – in time, in place, in setting.

For the most part, then, the sociologist obviates the problem of traits by viewing them as aspects of roles. We are what we have to be, and the grace with which it pleases us to accept the fact may well define the margins of what is 'personal' about traits. But suppose we turn the question about: If we begin with the psychological view that man is a bundle of traits, the assortment and allocation of which evolve dependably and predictably through social institutions, should we not then be able to match men and their traits with organizations and their requirements?

Needless to say, role theory itself compels us to answer that this ability to match is an entirely plausible view (after all, societies function and people do perform), conceived in muddled terms. Men are not composed of traits; psychology books are. The muddledness of the terms may account for the ambiguity of results when we set about unbundling traits. Traits are traps, capturing just enough real-life behaviour to cripple us permanently. That personality tests have not attained the glory of their promise may be laid to human imperfection, the deficient devices, or to the plain impossibility of the assumptions that inspired them. Yet matching men to organizations proceeds neither by chance nor by trait evaluations, and the best predictions are based on performance, not on the attitudes and preferences that accompany it.

Role theory, then, explains the disparity between social and psychological types on the ground that different tasks and purposes are involved. Roles imply trait selection but not the kind that comprise clinical psychological types. The counterpart of the psychologically requisite trait, desirable or undesirable, is a social demand – in short, a role through which that trait is realized. There is another reason, too, for the disparity between psychological and social types. The former are built about unitary and consistent sets of traits that are maintained only with difficulty under modern conditions of life. Such pure types do emerge, but they are infrequent. But the preference for describing behaviours rather than traits has by no means effaced the trait concept. As an idea, traits can be moved about and attached, so to speak, variously: as traits of person, as traits required by role, or simply as qualifiers of behaviour. If we are properly socialized, traits should indeed appear to be our very own.

Role or situation or person illuminate traits from different viewpoints; but in providing various points of reference, the analysis of traits is made more complex and even ambiguous. An instance is provided by the research on trust and suspicion in experimental game situations (Deutsch, 1958). Initially the terms imply a trait possessed; the game procedures suggest that the trait may vary with the situation, including the orientation of players as well as the conditions of the game itself. Both prove true. Deutsch found that trusting and trustworthy subjects conduced trust in others. In addition, by varying the game situation or the attitude of the other player, trust and suspicion may alternately emerge (Solomon, 1960). But are trust and suspicion 'traits'? They may be. Apparently, if we mean by trait a stable and consistent behaviour, they do not qualify as traits: if we define a trait as behaviour that more or less consistently varies with the situation, however, trust and suspicion qualify as traits. It is not their location in the person that has changed but the redefinition of the person. He is still the bearer of traits, though he hardly possesses them, for the trait emerges as a response within a situation. Hopefully, we look for sources of uniformity within role and situation; we do so because we can no longer easily find them inside the person.

7

Role and Self

W E have pointed to the way in which, for analytic research purposes, the theoretically conceived unity of 'mind, self and society' was split into its component parts, and it remains for us to indicate its focus on the 'self'. Role, we have seen, was largely converted into a formal, socially defined principle – given, objective and extrinsic. What, then, was conceived as intrinsic, and how was it defined?

Basically, two answers have been suggested. One is to view the self as strictly reflexive; i.e. it is simply the subjective aspect of role or role experiences, unified (or disunified), assimilated harmoniously (or unharmoniously), a composite of images, 'reflected appraisals' but also individual responses to those images and appraisals. In such a view, the self becomes fluid, its boundaries are shifting and uncertain, and we find here the origin of the so-called identity crisis. Second, the self may be viewed in strict autonomy. It remains the residual realm of individualism and freedom, of the spontaneous and impulsive, of all that has not been absorbed in social process and participation. This autonomy is the refuge of idealisms both old and new, of psychological theories of voluntarism and self-realization as well as religious (personalism) and philosophic (phenomenology, existentialism) doctrines. While the last view remains a renascent source of ethical and practical criticism, it presently furnishes few researchable propositions within the framework of current social-psychological enterprise. What, then, is the self the social psychologist talks about?

Modern man, conscripted into many roles, reflects objective diversity and complexity. He becomes many-sided; he is 'all things to all people'; his unifying or central features become problematic, and consequently the self becomes a diffused and uncertain abstraction. Moreover, this diffusion has been accentuated by most modern psychologies of personality, too, where we meet it as psychic complexity resulting in a tentative equilibrium. Where the self is divided into component parts as strata, its conflicts become a war of the self with itself. This discordant self with its many paradoxes of unity and integration typifies all modern theories, although it was first presented as a revolutionary discovery within psychology. Generally there has been a tendency for social theorists not to disparage so much as to set in social context the embattled self; it is an effort to put right the unnatural reification of psychologies of self. Only the *de facto* division of man into roles could explain his psychic partition, it might be argued; and only the social accentuation of inner and outer, private and public selves could produce such an exaggerated concern with aspects that were split off and called the inner self.

Only by expeditiously using what was already consummated in social experience could such a self become a researchable proposition. We cannot know, perhaps we do not have the right arrogantly to claim the 'whole man'. Thus, we focus on different aspects or levels of behaviour; so with 'mind', some of whose functions are translatable into cognitive or perceptual process, and so with 'person', whose exploration yields aspects or sides, layers or regions.

The radical redefinition of the self that role theory implied but never consummated has been resolved into three quite ordinary propositions.

1. At one extreme, the self is known only by visible and external behaviours. It is simply the individual aspect of every social act (behaviourism).

2. The self is conceived as complex fusion of internal and

external aspects of the social act. The I, the Me, the generalized Other represent both social process and an inner response to that process (G. H. Mead).

3. The self is regarded as an illusion. Technically, only imagery remains: either an idea of how a role is to be played (projection and presentation), or an idea about others' reactions to that role playing (self-image, as explained by Goffman).

We may say of (1), behaviourism, that its surface merits can hardly be avoided. Preoccupation with the covert and the hidden often makes us overlook the fact that our first point of reference has always been to objective aspects of person. These aspects include not only socially factual data like sex or age or occupation; they include all those aspects of person-as-object that are invisible or meaningless to the person but not to others. Gestures, expressive movements, accidental or mistaken 'meanings' are all hidden to one's self, not to others. For this reason, their interpretation and their meaning has necessarily to be one-sided. The person does not know, does not see himself as others do until he is told. The modern view that what is most significant about the person is hidden or obscure does not, needless to say, belong to sociology.

While (1) and (3) sound alike, analytically the procedures differ greatly. The surface realism of the one gives way to the systematic unravelling of illusion and masquerade, fiction and artifice, ritual and function in social life. (Social life does not lack depth, but people do.) But our interest here is in the dénouement of a self (2) that retains inner aspects.

We have suggested that the success of social behaviourism depended on a sundering of Mead's original theory. As a doctrine, the major influence of social behaviourism can be traced through large portions of small group research. The analysis of external acts and the coding of communication proceeds objectively: surface meanings are recorded, participants mean what they say, and sayings add up to functional role. The subjective parallel is obscured within the act of communication itself. It is there, but we cannot pay it full cognizance; and to this deficiency we often give tribute in vague references to 'personality' factors. Yet there have been many separate attempts in social psychology to recapture the subjective and covert aspects of the social act.

These aspects cannot be caught in process. In interaction analysis, the self merges into role, and therefore, for purposes of research, the self has been artificially removed from the social contexts that give it meaning. If, so reconstituted, it has more shadow than substance, we should not be altogether surprised. Precisely because it has been approached separately and obliquely (for example, as measures of feeling and attitude) and passively (how did you . . . or would you feel), an air of unreality, and sometimes triviality, accompanies it. Nonetheless, while such measures are never fully satisfactory, they preclude the complete evanescence of introspective self-aspects into the social self and, in their way, keep alive otherwise foregone I-aspects of the theory. In that theory we can be assured only where there is a unity of intention and act and meaning. The assumption is that such common meaning always emerges in social process; but if this were true, deception, hypocrisy, misunderstanding and error would be rare instead of common events. It is, therefore, the right to be heard, the right to question the apparent presentation of social life that matters. Unless we canvass all possible sides of role and interaction, we have access only to common meanings and appearances.

Investigations into subjectivity have given us measures like the following:

1. Image of self – who one thinks one is (for example, the 'Who am I?' tests, autobiographic measures, and self-rating scales);

2. Self as seen by others (rating scales, sociometric preferences);

3. Self as one thinks others see one;

4. Others seen like self (empathy, assumed similarity).

To many, of course, these measures seem partial and unsatisfactory. Generally, correlations between self-other images are only moderate; those between self as seen by self and as he thinks others see him are somewhat higher. (A summary of many of these measures may be found in Secord and Backman, 1964, pp. 579–90.) Curiously, instead of making self-experience more understandable, it becomes elusive. What, then, happens when subject becomes object, when the self is treated like any other person?

Suppose we begin first with what is generally called 'person perception' in social psychology. Early researches into how we perceive others were concerned with standard errors, systematic bias, and the inaccuracies of individual judgement. The large literature on impression formation, the halo effect, or the leniency effect demonstrated sources of common error by manipulating cues to which subjects more or less uniformly responded. It is not that the judgements of subjects were based on error or bias or stereotype that concerns us just now, however (though it was hardly incidental) – it is the fact of their agreement.

If our perceptions of others are highly categorical and conventional, what of our perceptions of ourselves? An individualist psychology hardly poses the question, because it presupposes uniqueness and introspective peculiarity – of course, the self is seen differently. It is more significant that a different type of research demonstrated not so much that the self was seen differently but that it was hardly seen at all. We recall here Werner Wolff's (1943) research into 'recognition of one's own personality'. In his experiments subjects were presented with a series of pictures, profiles and handwriting samples that included their own. Generally, subjects failed to recognize their own voices, their own hands, and usually their own handwriting and profiles. We may note that a puzzling exception was high self-recognition of gait. Apropos his findings he remarked: 'There are two general schools of opinion about the value of man's self-evaluation. One group believes man is nearest to himself: he knows himself better than anyone else does. The other group objects: Man is really farthest from himself; he knows himself less than do others' (p. 140). Wolff was convinced that both propositions contained some truth, for he had to explain, in addition, his finding that even though subjects failed to recognize themselves, they tended to make more extreme and emotional judgements when coming upon themselves in a series presented for judgement. He called this 'unconscious self-evaluation'.

To these problems social behaviourism has added its own interpretations. If our perceptions of others are socially learned, is not the perception of the self also? Should not each of us share in a consensus here, too, since we have all learned first to see ourselves as others and then later to see ourselves as others see us? This was the socially determined self of social behaviourism, and it came to be a dominant conception in numerous investigations of the self – of placement and rating, of liking and esteem. Assumed similarity, empathy and congruency are more recent terms that describe how the social self is psychologically linked to social milieu. All are attempts to explain elements of consistency and stability of self-image whether we are or are not as others see us.

Properly, of course, contrast should be drawn between different approaches then and now. For individual psychology, the research indicated discrepancies: why, as Wolff put it, 'the self judgement is definitely different from judgement by others' (albeit unconsciously). For social psychology the question was one of harmony, that is to say, how we learn to see ourselves as others do. The one approach was that of individual experience, the other of social experience that might or might not confirm the self-image. In the first view, the self is given; in the second it emerges and the differentiation of the self into 'images' and 'counter-images' encompasses most of the inconsistencies that had been a problem for individual psychology.

Nonetheless, the assumption of harmony between self and others, or of self and society, has not proved altogether easy. The key issue for individual psychology was how to account for the remarkable coalescence of mind and society, and for a long time so-called 'social perception' lent itself to the language of 'salience' (of object) and 'selectivity' (of subject)

so that all interpretations paraded through innumerable individual minds. Today proponents of a social theory of the
self have to explain other discrepancies by emphasizing a self
divided and fragmented by inconsistent social experiences.

We have to admit that the empirical self presents troublesome data. Logically, the self disappears once it is treated
like other objects; empirically, subjects have difficulty recognizing themselves. We are now alert to the defences of error
and misperception and rationalization on the part of the
subject; and we are well aware of how difficult it can be for
harmonious selves to emerge in a pluralistic, role-divided
world. Yet it is just these disharmonies and discrepancies
that suggest why we continue to pay attention to self data.
We have to acknowledge that very often recognition and
judgement and perception offer different perspectives when
seen by self and others. It is because we do not yet know the
rules for their correspondence (or noncorrespondence) that
we attend both sets of data.

The self – visible and invisible – has been well explored,
and yet its very exploration has distanced us from the conceptions with which we began. The fragmentation of the
person we regard today as socially and psychologically
natural at once makes possible research into self and person
and at the same time virtually precludes our ever quite putting him together again. Only in this fragmentation, it may
be suspected, lies whatever vestige of obscurity and mystery
remains. From this standpoint, large portions of explorations into subjectivity – from attitude studies to empathy
scales, from assumed similarity to preference ratings, from
taped psychotherapy sessions to photographed toilet and sex
behaviours – appear as the progressive denudation of person
for research purposes, whose counterpart is the collapse of
traditional conceptions of the hidden and the private. What
remains of the self? If the hitherto invisible becomes visible
and all hidden knowledge public, the radical redefinition of
the self is no longer new, it is simply irrelevant. The mystery
of persons is no more than the veil of privacy and ignorance
– in short, no great mystery at all.

It is hardly surprising that new definitions of conflict and crisis have emerged from the role literature or that the new refraction of the self has engendered a cluster of ideas whose references are interpersonal rather than personal, social rather than individual. Among the favoured attacks on the 'old self' is the illusoriness of the dimension called 'depth' or the importance we ascribe to it. The hidden, the disguised, the repressed and the rationalized all lend depth but are by no means the exclusive sources of complexity. Such sources may also be derived from the analysis of interaction itself. Consider, for example, Simmel's comparisons from the standpoint of one variable, that of number and the effect of 'adding one' in the analysis of dyads and triads. Analyses of role-sets (Merton) or interlocking roles, role distance (Goffman), or the dynamics of role reversal furnish other instances.

Role reversal, rather little accounted in the onrush of interaction analysis, is perhaps the most interesting of all. Here things are never as they seem, because movement within the role relation produces an inversion of roles. Such role reversals have provided us with certain ironies of everyday life as well as high drama: a favoured example is the case of master and servant, because the one depends on his own efforts and so becomes self-reliant while the other becomes dependent. There are other examples, such as the popular leader who must follow the led, or the *aperçu* that 'one always takes on the face of one's opponent'. While such ideas should serve as a corrective to devotees of formal role analysis, they remain difficult to work with. Where the inner content of a relationship may signify the opposite of its external form, the identification of role with mask, masquerade, or façade is given yet another dimension in its somewhat complex history.

The analysis of roles in depth may be quite useful but is little used, and much more typical is the derivation of complexity out of role multiplicity. It is the character of our lives that matters here – the diverse and multi-faceted person, or the complex personality, has got that way because he is a carrier of many roles. The crises and conflicts he experiences, therefore, belong to a way of life. In short, it is no longer an inner drama we attend but an external one, and we call it role conflict.

Perhaps no greater clamour has surrounded any of numerous variations on this theme than the type of role conflict called the identity crisis with its commingling of old personality theory and role analysis.

Since identity crisis exemplifies very well some contrasting uses of role conflict as a psychological and as a sociological idea, we may turn first to it. Both ideas recognize that the problem of identity has much to do with social setting: modern society presents us with many possibilities of role and identification. Both recognize, too, that the core of the problem is related to successful internalization (what to identify with). Moreover, in both views the symptoms are agreed upon: in the presence of choice, there is an incapacity to choose, in the presence of decision, indecisiveness; hence, distance, indifference, and noninvolvement become signs of personal and social crisis. Role definition from a psychological standpoint is treated as an aspect of personality, external to it and hence essentially an ego-achievement, a problem of mastery and integration (Erikson). The sociological view is rather different. Since a condition of modern life is uncertainty and apparent choice where formerly life was limited, ordered, or arranged for us, we can objectively view the problem of identity as a surfeit of choice over desire and as aimlessness in the absence of definite, learned aims. In the first, questions of autonomy and integration loom large because psycho-biological needs are still central; in the other, questions of risk, uncertainty and anxiety prevail because socially defined needs or aims have been removed. In the one view, strong egos choose; in the other, secure and stable role learning has occurred. Questions of distance or attachment to role, or technical problems of competence and management, can be resolved through either set of terms.

Yet what is subjectively called an identity crisis – the unresolved conflict over acceptance and rejection of roles – tends to mask the fact that we are no longer dealing with an individual peculiarity but an invalid state of whole groups. Originally age-linked, it was first used to explain the youth crisis. If the vicissitudes of different developmental stages were weathered, then integrated selves emerged; but their frequent upset suggested that more was involved than the fortuities of the individual life history. Nor did identity problems appear to be simply an affliction of youth. Groups are differently exposed, and whole segments of the population might be said to be prone to one kind of identity conflict or another – the retired old as well as the occupationless young, women, ethnic groups, and so on. Hence, the broader terms of role conflict are more often used today in describing typical crises incumbent upon particular group positions against which particular individual problems emerge.

In theory, all questions of strong egos, of unity and integration, can be made to depend upon one's good fortune in role learning. Role learning combined with psychoanalytic theory may make that learning depend upon the quality and kind of cathexis that has characterized our attachment to others (Parsons). It may go further and explain thereby the psychic disposition to conform to or be alienated from the social system. But it cannot explain massive failures in the articulation of individual and social systems where the identity, function and role of whole groups is at stake; nor is it relevant to the genesis of conflict associated with marginal role positions.

The social sources and the social indices of role conflict by no means necessarily correspond to the psychological experience of conflict. Their coalescence in the identity crisis has served to obscure the fact that similar symptoms are not uniformly displayed so that criteria for the definition of conflict must be sought outside the person's awareness of discomfort. Role conflict may or may not be displayed in aimlessness or disaffection or indecision; such problems are of social-psychological (rather than clinical) interest when they can be given a social location, when they typify particular social positions that involve conflicting demands, or when they can be shown to be role-bound.

142

8

Criticisms of Role Analysis

WHILE the most durable criticism personality theory has brought to role analysis has been the disappearance of person into role and institutional function, similar alarums have not infrequently been raised by sociologists themselves. It is the dismal and prosaic picture of the overdetermined world of man that has most often been attacked – a world whose theatricality has been limited to unimaginative stage sets, roles, and interactions of the 'same old scenes', thus leaving scant room for personal whim or individual freedom. Here all personal features are removed from the realm of the individual as strength of character or sphere of freedom and relocated as routine possibilities or limitations of roles within given social structures. And here even the illusion of self is seen as no more than a pronouncement of the success of internalized norms: we appropriate as personal qualities those aspects of roles we have learned to honour or to censure according to their social uses. Perhaps the harshest criticism of this sort has come from Ralf Dahrendorf (1968) who has given to this sociological model the name 'homo sociologicus'. He is, as Dahrendorf has elsewhere observed, 'a horrible character'. The tight, formal analyses of role theory when associated with functionalism and systematic sociology often turn that character into caricature. There are few aspects of social life – too few, as some see it – that are not fitted firmly together. Generally, life is quite predictable, movement is prescribed, and all vitality pre-empted. Theoretically, roles

F   143

may be vehicles of realization and fulfilment as well as restriction and restraint; but if so, the latter emphasis has been pushed with such proponent zeal that we can scarcely acknowledge other possibilities.

Into roles we are born, through others we live, and in others we die. In this unremitting cycle of roles, there is no escape. Whatever we do or do not do a role is there waiting for us: the theory provides myriad designations for would-be role escapees. In short, even the most cursory review suggests how it has come about that these doctrines, in theory and in fact, can only breed *révoltés* – revolutionaries in spirit if not in fact.

If we ask why spontaneous, autonomous, or self-affirming acts tend to be identified as role denials, we would point first to the difficulties of a theory of motivation too firmly allied to role theory. *Motives are always embedded in roles.* In such a structure of motivation, role acceptance, for whatever reason, is always objective compliance; contrarily, the appearance of freedom can come only through objective noncompliance with role demands – it must be acted out. Officially, we have the language of deviation and with it the cataloguing of varieties of role rejection – sometimes presented as forms of '*anomie*' (Merton) or 'alienation' (Parsons).

Technically, they should not be dubbed rejections, for we have simply eschewed some roles and elected others. There is no opting out. What is called role rejection is not just rejection but a negatively evaluated or penalty-carrying role. Closer scrutiny suggests that the exercise of choice may or may not be relevant; but if we equate rejection with freedom and choice, it is easy to mistake all role rejections as freely chosen. Perhaps one of the most puzzling features of functionalist theory is the 'functional equality' of deviants. We all know that neither hobos, beatniks and bohemians, nor the ill, nor the criminal form a homogeneous group against role conventions; yet all such roles are cast together as forms of deviation or rejection, of alienation from or nonarticulation with institutional requirements. Conformity and nonconformity become issues once again.

144

Sometimes efforts have been made to allow for unstructured motives, for idiosyncratic and chance effects. They are hardly apt correctives for a social system conceived to revolve about the central concerns of allocation and fit, nor is it likely to appease those critics who protest its total conceptions and seemingly preternatural delight in a system where all is known and all is interpretable. Therefore, it is important to ask precisely at what point allowance has been made for distance between motive and role, expectation, demand, and performance, and the play of personal effects.

As social psychologies go, two general solutions have been put forth: one is to emphasize variations in role performance; the other is to extricate the structure of motivation from its tight bondage with role.

We may distinguish first those social-psychological theories that have focused on variations in role performance. Here the problem is resolved in a way made quite familiar by old 'expressive' theories of personality. In both instances, personality is really no more than stylistic variation, but in the one we attach these variations as qualities of the person, whereas in the other we objectify them and speak of stylistic variations in performance. Instead of looking for core or nuclear traits, we look at what the person does and accordingly reinterpret all subtleties of personality as describable variations in presentation and performance of roles. Interesting discrepancies between theory and practice, intention and act, or peculiarities of approach and avoidance, as well as consistency and inconsistency, could be accounted here. The strictly conventional, adaptive, or superficial aspects are presumably of no great concern but at once point to certain difficulties. Many, if not most, stylistic variations are recognizably group- and class-bound. Far from being discernibly individualistic, our identification of others is almost always a summary role placement. We categorize; we stereotype; unerringly, we 'place' others.

Hence, stylistic variation does not appear to be the reliable source of individuality some have thought it to be. It has, in fact, been suggested that most personality ploys are simply

145

techniques we use to polish off good or bad performances. Thus Goffman (1972) has hypothesized that it is primarily in manifestations of 'role distance' that personality is to be found; and we may consider momentarily what he calls its manifestations. Role distance is intended, of course, to include all stylistic variations, for it covers the variety of rituals by which we cover, disguise, smooth over or accommodate ourselves to difficult or embarrassing performances. These thoroughly familiar devices – from *politesse* to jocularity, stand-offishness to conversational niceties – are not so much personal as socially available techniques for 'getting on with the show'. Personally pre-empted, they become identified with individuals or types of individuals. But role distance also includes the creation of effects in the theatrical sense of manoeuvre and manipulation of a 'bad scene'. This may mean 'playing at' a role (superficial involvement and posing), 'putting on' (clowning), underplaying (disparagement) or overplaying (perverse or exaggerated take-offs). According to this conception, it might well seem that personality is not so much used to express a self as to conceal it.

Lest we suppose that such concealment is primarily significant by virtue of either ego-protective or ego-enhancing functions, we should perhaps set straight at once its sociological message. Egos require either protection or enhancement not out of inner necessity but out of the social contexts that lend them meaning. Ultimately we must see that meaning as participatory: social life is a game with rules we share. Hence, team performance and keeping the show going are kindred terms for the ongoingness and unstable equilibrium of social life. The same concern appears in exchange theories as tendency towards equalization or maintaining the reciprocity rule, and in functionalist doctrines where the linkage between motivation and role keeps the system going.

Finally, and perhaps most favoured of all, is the resolution of personality variation through multiple role-taking. We should place here all those doctrines that emphasize role diversity, the peculiarities of role conflict and its resolution, competence, management, and the harmonious handling of different roles.* Still visualized here are elements of choice, selectivity and deliberation, and of a kind of harmony and balance that have long been extolled in traditional personality theories. These elements remain despite the fact that many priorities and options appear to have a strong social and conventional base and appear remote indeed from the exercise of individual choice. Significantly, choice involves alternatives to two aspects of old personality theory that role analysis most vigorously attacks: in place of unity and consistency it offers explanation of diversity and adaptiveness; and instead of uniqueness, it suggests the realistic limits of role repertoires from which some choice can be made. If we consider the possible sources of richness or diversity or extraordinariness of person, we may well eschew romantic notions of depth and hidden complexity and all mystery of person as such. But we cannot eschew the possibility of idiosyncratic assimilation of role experiences, of extraordinary roles, of the effects of diversification, or of role specialization to the point of virtuoso performance. All of these 'make' personality, and we duly acknowledge them.

Important as these views have been, they have only partially allayed dissatisfaction with the terms of analysis. We should not underestimate the significance of redefinitions that made us see and relocate the self's attributes, that permitted us to view its external and shared features, and so corrected our impulse to relate everything to the small world of the self. It is useful to know that an actor cannot be separated from setting and prop without appearing absurd, to be shown that we know others not in themselves but through the situations and contexts in which they appear. There is no bureaucrat without his office, no teacher without classroom, no father without his household. Yet it is true that in fitting

* We should include here also D. Emmet's use of the principle of 'detachment' (though the context in which she uses it is that of freedom from 'role bondage') to counter the view of person as merely an assemblage of roles. See *Rules, Roles and Relations* (1966), pp. 170ff.

closely together role, situation and setting, we were often given simply reverse propositions to old personality theory. All of the accoutrements of person, formerly located 'inside', were shifted to the 'outside', leaving us the critical problems of individuality and deviation when inside and outside did not converge as harmoniously as the theory supposed.

The real difficulty of the theory lies not in the sacrifice of person to system, not in the denigration of personality to the management of style or techniques of presentation, nor in the summation of person into roles. The inseparability of the person from his roles is nowhere more apparent than when we actually set about trying it. It is, rather, that the cultural world of roles encourages us to attend external performance, the mechanics of successful staging and the analysis of inter-action as if thereby we exhausted the meaning of the act. Its contrary assumption is that all significance is revealed there, that there is an identity of meaning between all persons and their acts, or if not such an identity, then a wilful collusion. But we know that things are not always as they appear and that perspectives and motives vary, giving us different meanings and interpretations of the same reality.

It is, therefore, the kind of emphasis that tightly binds the structure of motivation to the structure of roles that bears re-examination. No play of personality, no stylistic effects, no mastery of manœuvre quite touches the matter.

The relation between motive and role is usually sufficiently close to provide us with most of the rules and regularities of social life. We meaningfully specify different motives and perspectives, then, as they vary with role and position. But there are also many points at which we must separate the two if we are to remain alert to all those disharmonies and dis-crepancies that fall outside the systematic, the uniform and the expected. The structure of motivation is not always defined by role. The same role may use various motives or a mixture of motives. One may yearn for profit and wealth but also be driven by a need for diligence and hard work. Motivation can be disguised through roles. Love of power or influence can be transmuted into the care and cure of others.

148

Above all, motivation has a history of its own.* Such is the individual side of role, whose objective appearance or function nonetheless presents the same face.

At this point the separation of behaviourism from its social base presents critical difficulties. If we return to Mead's basic principle that society is built upon common meanings and the sharing of significant symbols, then it follows that all breakdowns of common meaning and discrepancies in the use of symbols by different users become key problems. Customarily, only individual and social crises force this to attention – such is surely the case today. Whether as motive or perspective, as interest or interest group, the individual and individualizing aspect of social act and social process has to be accounted. All is not necessarily revealed in the act: we never know unless, like the courts of the land, we establish procedures for deciding whether the same act is accident or murder, innocence or wilful deception, ignorance or fraud.

The collapse of fixed rules is intimately tied to a felt crisis of roles; both imply a changed content and meaning for different groups, and an unnatural haste to establish general rules leaves us with unsolved problems of variance, conflict, and deviation – things that 'do not fit'. Hence, there has arisen the quite standard criticism of role theory as inflexible and the role system as a closed system unless upset by perturbations external, alien, and devious to it. It is to this matter that we turn next, for it is true that social change has put in question certain suppositions upon which role theory has been based and that, inevitably, it poses threats to the stable picture of any given role structure.

* The last, of course, can be used to summarize all that we need to observe. Gerth and Mills (1954) have used the personal history – 'biography' in their text – to make room for these discontinuities. It remains one of the few statements to stand apart from formal systems theory without disintegrating all theory.

PART III

Change

9

Change: Social and Individual

WE come upon one of the touchiest of areas. As we know, a common criticism of role and role-systems theory has been its limited capacity to explain change within and its total incapacity to anticipate change from without. Strange as some of these allegations are – for system analysis has enhanced our awareness of multiple sources of change, and a large part of role analysis has been devoted to interpreting our experience of social change – we shall examine them in some detail. All in all, our views have become more differentiated, and we hedge our explanations. Change is not more ubiquitous than in former times; but its diffusion is more rapid, our consciousness of it more acute, and our explanations more complex. We search and research what was once God's will (finding cloud-seeding more rewarding than prayers); and bypassing faith in evolution and the natural course of events, we would speed history by investing in technology (the development of underdeveloped nations), controlling population and the like – planful as our knowledge permits us to be, but hardly omniscient.

There are a number of academic conventions surrounding discussions of social change that we may recapitulate briefly here. A basic distinction is usually drawn between qualitative and quantitative descriptions of change. The first gives us the classic typologies of social history: *gemeinschaft* and *gesellschaft*, status and contract, folk society and civilization. They are qualitative in that they describe two contrasting ways of life: the one traditional, solidary, status-bound, and relatively undifferentiated; the other modern, differentiated, class-bound, and built upon the division of labour and an elaborate technology. Currently, this qualitative contrast has been absorbed into the theory of the modern, that is to say, the great leap forward from backward to civilized, under-developed to developed, primitive to industrial social systems. While the theory has developed in the wake of standard nineteenth-century evolutionary theory and is often contrasted to it, the affinity between the two is pronounced. In both instances history is, so to speak, given a push: it is ascribed movement and direction; and, of course, Western societies remain the established model of change. Quantitative descriptions typically provide the data for the theory of the modern, and a variety of measures from vital statistics to industrialization, urbanization to changed attitudes and beliefs forms its content. The model has been summarized this way:

The essential character of the assumptions underlying most of the discussion of industrialization may be summarized by three interrelated but analytically separable positions:

1. Economic transformation is viewed as the intermediate phase of a three-stage model of social transformation: (a) a static, pre-industrial stage, (b) a dynamic transitional stage, and (c) a static state following the 'industrial revolution'.

2. During transition, industrialism is viewed as an externally induced system that has a problematic impact on the presumably static and resistant traditional structure. Structural analysis is used to trace through the consequences of the new set of social elements, but only rarely is attention given to the interaction of structures in juxtaposition, and the resulting modification of the structure of industrialism.

3. Although antecedent cultures are conceded to be widely diverse the process of industrialization is viewed as leading to a common destination. When the transition is complete, the required structural changes in social systems will have been made, the boxes will be 'filled in', and the post-industrial societies, implicitly static, are explicitly alike [W. E. Moore (1967)].

So it is to be one world after all. It used to be common to differentiate types of determinism in different theories of social change; but only one remains, the economic. It was formerly customary to specify the direction of change in time (evolutionary and cyclic theories); the question is submerged in the new theory as if there could be no turning back. Old theories of the direction of change in space (diffusion) are acknowledged to be too simple. Multiple and complex relationships are obtained between cultural spheres. Nonetheless, like some older theories, economic and technical matters remain at the heart of the theory, while the notion of a pattern of diffusion had to be foregone.

To see the difficulty of tracing a standard pattern of diffusion, we may digress momentarily on one popular theory of innovation of the recent past, that of Ogburn and his associates (Ogburn and Gilfillan, 1933). Of course, so highly technological is our orientation and so accustomed are we to ascribing the weight of social change to the sphere of technology that we are likely to regard all significant change as technological and assume that all technological change necessarily involves social change. Ogburn has to remind us that innovation refers not just to technical inventions but social ones like 'the city manager form of government, the chain store, esperanto, and basketball'. Still, most of the examples used were technical ones and, since the notion of culture lag (uneven adjustment to new invention) is identified with his work, the whole theory has had a technological ring to it.

According to Ogburn, the tracing of change effects throughout society should have followed upon his theory of diffusion, according to which those effects could be traced 'like a pebble thrown in water'. Of course, no such orderly tracing was possible either then or now, and if we follow his work, it seems to follow instead a kind of 'culture wheel', each spoke of the wheel representing a visible consequence in a particular social sphere. Sometimes he spoke of a fan in reference to the spreading out of effects, sometimes of chain effects. The mixture of metaphors conveys the many difficulties faced in trying to establish an orderly sequence. Today we simply group these together as second-order effects.

Suppose we take a list of such effects, the following being a sample, and without specifying what invention he referred to, try to guess what it is that:

aided the growth of suburbs
affected the size of villages
reduced railroad traffic
changed the hotel business
modified manners and morals
increased crime
diminished the employment of domestic servants
consolidated schools
changed marketing areas
caused international difficulties over oil resources.

The aeroplane? the diesel engine? the automobile? radio? television? Any one of these might be matched to the list, but the reference was the automobile. Today we would greatly expand the list, particularly into areas of public safety and public health, quite unforeseeable at the time of writing. What the exercise does show us is how we have to be humbled by the complexity of change effects. The above list represents not single-order effects but multiple ones from different sources than the automobile. We have come to regard diffuse effects and cross-effects as typical, but they also preclude our establishing orderly patterns or sequences of change. Moreover, the eye is not all-discerning. We cannot capture many of the dimensions of change in time and space even for single inventions. Distant and delayed effects (in time) or hidden and invisible ones (in space) cannot be assessed. We are faced with an iceberg of data only half of whose features are visible, and we have simply retreated to more manageable problems. The iceberg analogy serves well to describe the present state of affairs: we have plenty of inventions that soar upward like rockets into the unknown, but their technical base has become so intricate that it is submerged knowledge for all but specialists. The social researcher has long since returned to his own data to describe and measure what has happened and is happening to society in the wake of change.

We can see in the modern theory of social change a convergence from different sources. Its qualitative aspect remains strong; its economic-technical focus is central; its ambition to measure the numerous, simultaneous effects of change is keener than ever. All of this is true whether the problem of change is that of the developing nation or of change in our own society. Of the latter, perhaps the best example is the recent tracing of second-order effects of space technology (Bauer *et al.*, 1969). Here, initially, second-order effects have to be differentiated. Space science, space technology and space exploration each carry their own sets of consequences but remain interrelated. Their social and economic effects, in turn, form a separate series. The complications appear excessive, but the researcher may begin with the first manifest social consequence of the space programme – in this case not the proliferation of research facilities or attendant industries but a new phenomenon that includes both: the space town. He then proceeds through community study and field survey techniques to depict the structure of the new town. Its accommodation to highly specialized purposes, its occupational structure, its recruits and its residential patterns give us the ecological picture. Mediating institutions and programmes in the schools and the community present another order of effects, attitude and opinion surveys still another. We have not yet necessarily gone far enough in tracing second-order effects. The study also includes an analysis of space argot and the diffusion of its language (technical and slang); and it could include, more than it does, other symbolic representations of the space programme in popular art. Far from being exhaustive, the survey is tentative, diffuse, and most interesting because it is a first step in a new field. There is no formal model through which it works; no claim to a complete or orderly depiction of social change; but it does provide a way into diversified data and problems as the researcher confronts them and into the many paths he may follow in describing aspects of change. Above all, it pulls together small-scale and large-scale change.

The last point is a major concern. Theories of social change are of considerable interest to social psychology and yet have remained remote. The essential social-psychological concern involves almost insuperable difficulties, for it centres not on the facts of change but how it comes about (what sets it in motion, who are its carriers), what its effects are (who gains, who loses; what moves forward, what recedes), and what rationale or attitudes accompany it. Hence, attention to the problems of social change means attention to the vicissitudes of particular groups. The ordinary data of social change – the sociologist's first concern – are but a point of departure. From this standpoint, as we shall see, the social-psychological aspects of change have been rather little examined. Formally speaking, they have been but slightly related to theories of change. Much of its material consists of residues that do not 'fit', of disorderly aspects of the social system, of social problems, and of a wide range of social movements. Such manifestations of instability have underscored the fact of social change without being coherently related to it. By hindsight we are reminded that real men and women enact social process, that behind the indices of social change are people whose experience of it is often expressed elsewhere, if not through the current institutional order, then interstitially or outside of it. Some examples are given in Table 9.1. Many of the consequences of institutional change, like the economics of the auto or of public health, are neither evasioned nor foreseen. Planning change is now organized (though clairvoyance is not), and this formal aspect is recognized as an institution in itself. Less popularly acknowledged, though much studied, are the many sources of change that represent adjustments between institutional spheres. The handiest examples are those between family and economy, whose tendency to become institutionalized (the 'welfare state') has constituted much of modern social history. Finally, as a source of change, there remain those 'alienative' groups that find no wedges in the institutional order. One way or another their attacks on that order have produced changes, not necessarily of the kind intended, but change nonetheless.

So much for the formal picture. Let us consider next the

ways in which the problem of change has been handled by different social psychologies.

Personality and Social Change

Awareness of the highly relative nature of research on social change, and even keener awareness of the complexities we attempt to interpret, stand in particularly strong contrast to psychological theories of the past. In the past, significant change was self-engendered, and change was interpreted in the primitive and intimate terms of personal will, desire, and deed. While today we regard such notions as wholly lacking in objectivity, nonetheless the linkage of the personality principle to a theory of social change has been an enduring feature of social psychology.

This linkage derives from the inherent capacities of person as well as from unpredictability or mystery of person, from factors of change and impulsivity as well as from individual variation and mutability. The philosophic idealism long associated with the personality principle is bound to its transcendent qualities – its presumed effectiveness beyond itself, its generative power, its restless movement within the conditions of social existence. The difficulty for social psychology was to distinguish restiveness from effective, changeful action, and personal illusion from objective possibilities for realizing power or freedom or desire – the ruling triumvirate of person.

In its simple and uncomplicated form, this linkage has been perpetuated through a theory of leadership and the emergence of great personalities capable of imposing themselves on events and men – in crude psychological terms, of seeing their private aims rewarded as public purposes. This doctrine has emerged, submerged and re-emerged so frequently that we may judge its present abeyance as temporary. Even so, we might observe that most psychologies maintain it in one form or another – the aggressive instinct having given way to the achievement motive and master sentiments to dominant needs – and that the language of character and personality is

159

Table 9.1. Typical Examples of Social Change

I. SOURCE: INSTITUTIONAL	CONSEQUENCE	ADJUSTMENT
Technical development: automobile	early displacement of horse and buggy later displacement of mass transport	transfer to new occupations
	'distress areas'; decline of coal-mining with new fuels development	relief measures
	urban 'transport crisis'; traffic problem	public transport subsidy; traffic control
	urban sprawl	suburbanization
	job–home distance widens	commuter pattern of life
	economic interest groups (highway, oil, gas lobbies)	
Public health measures and medical practice	increased longevity	
	rise of 'population problem'	birth control movement
	increase in occupationless aged	social security programme; age interest groups
	economic markets for the aged sector	retirement housing projects; medical insurance

Institutional 'change agents'	industrial organization of research and development	organizational prestige as against independence
	decline of inventor	
	patent holding	purchase of patents; security for inventors
	industrial espionage	

II. SOURCE: INTERSTITIAL (THE 'VOLUNTARY ORGANIZATION')	CONSEQUENCE	ADJUSTMENT
Insecurity of small consumer as employee without independent resources	cooperative and mutual-aid plans in food, housing, medical care	the cooperative society; group health
Powerlessness of small local groups	grass roots movements; inner city neighbourhood projects	the community centre
Ameliorative efforts on behalf of deprived lower classes	private organization of social services	the settlement house
	adjustment and counselling programmes	the guidance centre

III. SOURCE: EXTRA-INSTITUTIONAL; UNCONVENTIONAL OR QUASI-ILLICIT GROUPS	CONSEQUENCE	ADJUSTMENT
Social target: the 'organization life'	new social movements: beat and hippie cults attack the impersonality and exchange values of organized social life, opt out of established role structure	hippie neighbourhood (the crash-pad and the free store) 'the commune'
	effects and influences: youth rights (love, drugs and politics), new styles (language, dress and decor)	
	new social movements: civil rights (aim: integration and equality)	political organization and support of interracial programmes, desegregation, fair employment statutes
Social target: the 'racist society'	Muslims and Panthers (aim: black separatism and resistance)	self-help programmes and neighbourhood defence units within the pluralist society

still drawn from a primitive arsenal of terms for aggression and defence.

In general, role analysis has reinterpreted all such self-affirming personality psychologies by stressing role prescriptions with their attendant limits and possibilities of action. Since historically roles change with social organization, it is usually regarded as less appropriate to speak of the downfall of individualism or personality in the modern world than to set the principle in context. Conquistadores, robber barons and entrepreneurs are not of our age; space heroes, corporate presidents and administrators are. From the standpoint of realizing power or freedom or desire, all are in an excellent position to advance or express their personalities, and some may even mistake this for their social function. If we want to contrast them as social types, reference to personality or self-realization or achievement is not very helpful. They belong to different settings and environments and are only comprehensible against the definitions of their time and place. They realize themselves in different ways.

Sociological theories leave scant room for heroes not by denying their existence but by setting the heroic in context and therefore seeing as limited (by time, place and circumstance) what others called the unlimited expression of self-affirmation and the will to power. This limitation is not simply because most role performances are routine, or because only some roles elicit heroism of any sort (convict subjects of medical experiments are not heroes, but a researcher who infects himself is), or because heroism of any sort is bound to the prestige order ('Mohawks in steel' versus astronauts), or because the idea of the heroic changes from time to time. It may also be observed that the general tenor of the world of roles discourages, it marks a profound shift of mood as well as perspective. Persons and things are put in place and in context while one scans the social field and defines social space, moving from the personal to the panoramic and back again. In doing so, the centrality of person is necessarily lost and therewith the self-justifying qualities of great personalities as agents and prime movers, heroes and chiefs.

163

Thus the notion of person as agent has largely receded as the accumulation of social data has risen. This change is hardly accidental. The growth of the social sciences in modern times has meant an emphasis on the collective, interrelated aspects of social life; on pluralism not on singularity; on cumulative, multiple effects not unilateral ones. Social data in this sense are as remote and distant as impersonal collective events like disasters, accidents or epidemics. Their distancing effects are all alike. If there were an attitude towards life, characteristically modern but comparable to the ancient idea of fate, brought down from the divine to the profane, it lies in the plight of the individual before uncontrollable, remote and often invisible events. The sociologist's structural sources of change are of this order of events, and the social change that is ascribed to structural factors (along with the linkage of social change to personal crisis) has come to be, perhaps more than we are aware, a dominant view. Change and the expectation of change is perhaps not distinctively modern, but the sense of crisis is, for we are far from the ancient benign doctrine that 'all is flux'; far, too, from notions of the divinely ordained; far again from the idea that societies periodically undergo critical turnovers called revolution. Instead we live with the view that change may be sudden or gradual, violent or peaceful, subtle or conspicuous, but is pervasive, inescapable, and unwilled.

In such a view social change, whether of a cataclysmic or cumulative sort, appears complex and impersonal, and the fate of the person is incidental to social process. It is something that happens to him. The facts of sociology or economics are impersonal, not because they do not derive from persons, but because they are the outcome of many single acts, wants or interests. The movement of people from one region to another gives us a migration rate, labour market data, differential age and sex distributions; it may also issue in special organizations for migrants and newcomers. People who 'live better' live longer; the fact of longevity for large numbers gives us differential age distribution in a population, retirement rules affecting the job market, social and political movements to protect the interests of the aged, and some new institutions provident of their needs. Now the tracing of multiple effects and interrelations removes us from the singular and the personal, but we confront people directly once again, not as facts or figures, rates or curves of distribution, but through organizations and institutions where they may be viewed individually or collectively. In moving full cycle from events to organizations to people, we return to individual actors or performers and the world of roles.

Change occasioned by great events or dislocations and by general trends and tendencies casts the person and his subjective experience into shadow. He is less actor than acted upon, less maker and doer than subject and sufferer. For sociological purposes, however, role as the unit connecting person to social order was admirably neutral in this respect. Whatever men were or were not thinking or feeling, functional shifts and changes in system and in institutions could account for changing roles. The fate of whole groups could be described largely in terms of such positions. The roles of women and children in relation to the industrial order, the impact of technology on job and occupational structure, and the adaptations of different minorities all serve as instances. There is no obscurity here: the social world, we are told, constantly changes, and the formal roles that connect the person to social institutions and organizations change, too, or give way, or disappear. Thus the sociologist's structural factors can be brought home as psychologically meaningful events, making personal quite impersonal matters through intermediary role constructs that serve to interpret the social world to men. The experience of crisis can be dovetailed with the theory of change. But how effectively has this been done?

Role Change

Often what is most protested in the overall theory is its concern with 'allocation' and 'fit' and its purely formal counter-concern with sources of disjunction and conflict. It is here, then, that the social psychology of roles should provide a corrective view. Theoretically, role analysis includes diverse sources of change: the very ongoingness of the acts contains the self-generative conditions for change through response and mutual adaptation, as can be shown in idle bits of conversation, the onset and crescendo of a quarrel, or the workings of an ordinary task group. But however general and pervasive the idea of change, the rules of interaction sharply modify it, and a search for equilibrium process has effectively circumscribed it. Therefore, it is often overlooked that a conspicuous portion of role propositions in social psychology involve hypotheses concerning role change. Consider the following:

1. From small-group research: If we change a person's position in a communication network, his activity and function change too (Bavelas and Leavitt).

2. From field research: If a person's occupational role changes, his attitudes and ideas will change in accommodation to that role (Lieberman's study (1956) of men who became shop stewards and supervisors).

3. From systematic sociology: Role change may occasion stress because new roles do not have established rules for 'scheduling' activities and obligations (Parsons). Contrast may be drawn between the established priorities of the old family physician (duty to patient) and the institutional physician with mixed duties in teaching, research and patient care, priorities not clearly defined.

4. From social theory: The assumption of new roles is probably facilitated by rituals of learning and indoctrination (Van Gennep on *rites de passage*).

Each of the above samples could be amplified by citing other portions of small-group research, of studies of role change, or investigations of 'secondary socialization' that substitute for ritual process the secularized learning of new roles (soldier, doctor, patient, prisoner, etc.). Finally, a specific type of role occupancy known as 'the marginal man' is defined solely in terms of its fluid, changeful aspects. The middle man, the stranger and the minority leader are go-between positions. Those who occupy them are in a position to introduce new modes or seek out new arrangements.

It will of course be noted that the terms of role conflict are either implicit or explicit in most of these propositions. The important question is: To what extent does conflict as a process generate change? In what measure do its terms provide leverage in an otherwise tightly constructed role system?

In sociology we speak of role conflict when different role expectations cannot be filled smoothly and satisfactorily by virtue of limits of time, energy or place (work versus play, job versus family, etc.); marginal position between two sets of relations (middle man); and transitional positions, movement from one situation or group to another (mobility upwards or downwards). Here role conflict is a product of role-sets, of multiple-role occupancy, and therefore of overlapping expectations. Customarily we emphasize its objective sources because the experience of conflict remains elusive and its resolution through denial or evasion commonplace; but there are graver difficulties.

All strains, tensions and frustrations can be related in some way to roles we play, but not all of them derive from conflicting role-sets and competing obligations. The tendency today is to subsume so much conflict as role conflict that the concept loses its capacity to differentiate. The intimate bickering of siblings or marriage partners is role-related but is not, in the above sense, role conflict. The appearance of indecisiveness does not give us an adequate criterion of conflict, merely of indecisiveness. Thus the eternal student or amateur or job shifter does not furnish a good example of role conflict; neither does the married woman who cannot decide whether she should work or stay at home. While strictly subjective, psychological definitions of role conflict have created problems here, they are problems of a consistent sort. Since only conflict that is felt or experienced matters, it becomes completely individualized and leads away from social psychology. Instead our question concerns the uses to which role conflict has been put social-psychologically.

In a systems presentation such as Parsons's (1952), role

conflict simply interacts, in a circular way, with other sources of deviance. Not only may the beginnings of role conflict have a remote source in early personal history (i.e. be 'ego made'), but, of course, there are sources in the social system itself that also predispose to 'alienative motivation'. In this thorough intermingling of subjective and objective role conflict, conflict becomes vague and diffuse, and the main mechanisms of change are largely located as defensive measures of social control. Rather few possibilities of change in line with the felt needs or claims of the alienated are envisioned. The sources of disjunction will be partially adjusted and the voices of disjunction quieted in the interests of system stability and equilibrium. We should not so much question the realism of this account as its formal, closed aspects. Change is mechanically adjustive or defensive, and there is overemphasis on the genesis of motives to conform or deviate that cannot account for large portions of deviance, just as there are many forms of deviance that have nothing to do with role conflict. Thus on the one side there are group positions, a reference to whose common experience lies not most meaningfully in their past history but in their present situation – the critical positions of the young and the old, for instance. These positions (critically tied to each other) cannot quite be construed in terms of a conflict of generations. To be sure, each represents certain conflicts of interest, and each stands in partial isolation from the economic order – the one presumably in preparation for available roles, the other in resignation from old ones. Yet the situations they face are largely the product of the changed facts of population itself, of technology and the availability of leisure, of shifting occupations and increasing stress on formal training and education.

Moreover, there are numerous groups, deviant from the norm, whose subcultural autonomy derives from role adjustment not role conflict, such as ethnic or sectarian groups. Their common experience as minorities, to be sure, rests on early learning and established identification with their own group. Their in-group adjustment sometimes, but not necessarily, occasions role conflict. Such groups accommodate in various ways, fill particular positions, and furnish standard illustrations of 'social symbiosis', not conflict. In the past, the successful Jewish or Quaker business man, the one willing to work on Sunday, the other investing in producers' goods instead of spending as a consumer, have been such examples. In short, the linkage of deviance to conflict is complex and provisional; both alike represent potential upsets but provide no theory of change. Deviance may involve little conflict on the one hand, or conflict little deviance on the other. There is nothing in the objective situation or in the formal definition of a conflict situation that moves it.

We are suggesting here that the propositions regarding change that might be associated in principle with role theory have largely vanished. This appears to be even more true when we compare the above theoretical formulations with recent research on role conflict. Objective definitions of conflict ('organizational stress') provide no hypotheses concerning processes of change, only a backdrop against which to measure individual responses to it. The work of Kahn and his associates (1964) is illustrative in this respect. To be sure, the setting within which role stress occurs is the formal organization (the plant, the office), and usually its rules and regulations are a major source of restriction and conflict. Here all potentially changeful elements within a conflict situation are gone, and statements about role conflict have come to be statements about 'frozen' positions of marginality – suggesting conflict without resolution and vacillation without direction. We are given accounts of play-offs, manœuvres and stalemates. Thus there is reflected a mood and a setting, describing the preconditions but not the urgency of change. The very old idea of the marginal man, whose exposure at boundary points predestines him for an innovative role, has quite given way. Instead there are bureaucratized men who occupy positions of conflict and others who occupy organization-designated roles devoted to change.

The absorption of role conflict into system theory, far from providing a theory of change, has given us functional principles of institutionalized conflict and has reaffirmed the idea of an unstable equilibrium whose counterpart is a social psychology of role crisis.*

Since the notion that there could be a theory of social change has long since been forgone, it is perhaps well to address the issues that are involved here. The problem of change lies not in the expected but the unexpected, not in the foreseen but the unforeseen. If our theories are too systematic or if they are too little so, we fault them alike. Yet if we look at the range of data, it becomes evident why the field remains fluid and empirical. The 'better' empirical data can be fitted securely into the model of a social system. Regular and irregular changes such as cycles and rates, and large-scale changes such as structural shifts and displacements generated in the economics of new products and new industries, serve as fitting examples. So true are these examples that the social system takes on the aspect of a fortress, as if its social planning and administration were all-provident and foreseeing. Change and changefulness are 'locked into' the system whether planned for or just happening as the sociologist discovers their correlates. Small-scale changes such as measuring interaction or group dynamics remain much more provisional, and we should note their case.

It has often been thought that change would or could be made more comprehensible by focusing on the small or limited case and following it step by step. Such studies – for example, the initiation of a new process in industry, the intro-

---

* Efforts to introduce nonsystem elements into the resolution of role conflict may be of interest here. This has been done by introducing apparent personality choices or styles in the handling of such conflict, i.e. correlating certain test scores with modes of conflict resolution. See, for example, S. Stouffer and J. Toby, 'Role Conflict and Personality' (1951), pp. 395–406, and E. Mishler, 'Personality Characteristics and the Resolution of Role Conflict' (1953), pp. 115–35. W. Goode's concept of 'role bargaining' (1960, pp. 483–96) introduces the idea of individual choice and balancing according to 'exchange rules'. In all of these instances the source of conflict resolution is located in the person by correlating his test scores or stated values with other choices and options he makes.

duction of fluoridation, or the placement of new drugs in the medical market – describe a process of change that decidedly removes all mystery. First, these are planned changes; second, their sponsorship makes them a kind of marketing problem that is not free and open but based on rational calculations and prearrangements. On the one side stand agents of change, on the other, receivers. The questions posed are much like those of market promotion, and the details are similar. How and where is the practice or product placed, who is influential in spreading it, who resists it; are there stages of change or transitional steps or a distributive curve to its spread? Useful and practical as such studies may be, their processing of expectable data is not the kind of problem we perhaps ordinarily think of as social change. It is, however, exactly the kind of planned change that has become familiar in daily life. Sometimes there are surprises in how plan and practice actually work out. For the most part, however, such studies are designed to sidestep the two aspects of change that are at once most troubling and most interesting: its latent or unforeseen side effects and its unpredictability. The researcher preconceives alternatives just as the planner plans for them, and the only message he can finally pronounce is one of success or failure. The true data of change in these instances, however, are the mistakes, missteps and failures – unplanned and uncalculated, one is prone to write them off. What is typically lost in the literature and research on social change is the inherently irrational element of change itself. Whatever surprises or upsets or alters our established and expected ways is just our ordinary conception of change, and to it we also often attach the label 'creative'.

We may cite as an example another kind of expertness that has often served in the planning of change. Anthropologists have long been called upon to provide information about native cultures that would ease the path of administered change. They could supply insight into expected difficulties or types of local resistance that might occur. The introduction of a new technique or a new crop, of sanitary and medical practices, of housing or transportation, has quite regularly conflicted with traditional spheres of religion, ritual and magic, of work customs or the sexual division of labour, and of food habits. The following excerpt relates to the medical practice of hospitalization – but consider its many overlapping features:

It is reported that in previous times in West Africa, the charms and talismans which gave a man the power to withstand evil forces were forcibly taken away from those hospitalized. In Burma, where villagers built one-storey houses to avoid having anyone over their heads, and where they slept on the floor to be certain that they would not break the rule against sleeping on a high place during the duty-days, the Western types of hospitals with their elevated beds could not have been reassuring to the ill. Where modesty or secretiveness attends evacuation, people find it harassing to use a bedpan. . . . In societies where all bodily effluvia are continuous with the body, to abandon phlegm, blood or excreta to strangers may well be a source of unease. The records which have to be kept in a hospital, with the large number of questions they involve, are reported as producing distress; the inquisitiveness is a source of worry, and even the capturing of the personal name in symbols on paper has produced fear in people who have to protect themselves against magic. Where part of the definition of a good doctor or diagnostician is that he should know everything, the questions make the incoming patient distrust the doctor who has to ask before he knows [M. Mead (1955), p. 207].

Similar scruples and concerns have centred on most cultural features introduced from outside so that finding an apt entry has been a paramount concern. One favoured way – the use of the local establishment – presents one of the most ambiguous aspects of change, one that generates a separate series of effects within planned change. It has been quite common to elicit native religious or ritual specialists to lead villagers to a vaccination programme in the name of old divinities, not modern medicine. In the same way, fitting established chiefdoms into a European administrative apparatus expedited the wielding of imperial power. Each in its own way might be said to have furnished an early education in nationalism. In both cases the use of native authorities might be seen as also providing validating experiences for later independence. From these ranks, the leadership of nativist or new nationalist movements might appear a natural development. And so it does, once it has occurred. Such unforeseen aspects of change far outweigh the immediate programmes that originally helped set them in motion; only much later can we pursue at leisure their multiple causes.

An important aspect of all modern planning has been the proliferation of its personnel (bureaucratization) and a sharp division between helper and helped. This aspect of the politics of planning has been full of surprises in the administration of both domestic poverty programmes and foreign projects. It has lead some observers to emphasize the hazards of too much planning:

> Practically all development projects today that are initiated among underprivileged people began in the offices of government ministries or foreign assistance agencies. Elaborate plans are drawn up by specialists . . . and after extensive negotiations are taken to selected areas. It is here that the problems begin since the gulf of understanding between the *élite* and the ultimate recipients may be enormous. And if the plans are minutely detailed before the period of interaction on the recipient level begins there may be very serious difficulties. The idea of 'self-help' is valid only when it also includes planning and decision-making by the recipients [Niehoff (1966), p. 77].

In our own time, zeal for planned change has been tempered by the knowledge that all cannot be planned and foreseen. Modern demographers never fail to remind us of the mixed blessings of enlightened public health and medical practices that have helped to create a population explosion; economists may emphasize the hazards of 'consumerism' in a society that has not yet settled its problems of poverty to make consumers of us all; political scientists may suggest the ease with which the welfare state passes into the authoritarian state in the disinterested interests of social peace.

Small-Scale Changes in Small Groups

We now return to the case of interaction process and group dynamics. Many of the problems of measurement of group process we have already touched upon elsewhere; here we should like to emphasize the fact that among the criticisms of such measurement is one that is similar to those mentioned above in connection with planned change. Interaction is inherently changeful and ongoing. If we focus on its rules or its equilibrium process, we cannot at the same time attend well its covert aspects or its momentary changefulness. Nor, might we add, are these necessarily of great interest; they are not to everyone. Just as in large social systems, so in small ones: the sources of change are various; some are susceptible to prediction because they repeatedly occur under like conditions (such as the unstable interaction process of the triad with its 'odd man out'), and some are not. What is lost is the spontaneous, unexpected, or uncodeable aspect of an interchange. For example, we may have to code collective laughter that shames or ridicules as tension-releasing as well as that which heartens. We do not code significant smiles or qualifying gestures or the language of the glance. Shifts in tone or level of interaction cannot be caught until they are consummated as a pattern. Such interaction data we can get at by other means (for example, observation or interview analysis) but not through small-system analysis. The creativity of the act, its occasional surprises or upsets, are lost to the code, the planned observation, and the social rule.

Why do we attend at all these sources of change? Are they not demonstrably insignificant compared to those we can know and predict? Yes and no. In answer we have to say that the essence of change (and decidedly so of creative change) is just what is not known in advance, not planned or calculated or expected. No social and social-psychological theory discounts this. In the past, personality theories located such sources of change within the creative or extraordinary person; social theories located them in a conjunction of events or interactions. Both have occasionally converged in a theory of social movements.

Social Change and Social Movements

In summarizing sources of change from different standpoints, as we do in Table 9.2, the place of collective movements is an end point involving historical interpretations whose relevance for social psychology is contingent and hypothetical. Potential sources of change that are not foreseeable have been viewed as arising from creative personalities or creative minorities, as spontaneously emerging from interaction process, or as ways of resolving conflict. From the standpoint of social systems, the question is one of balance between mechanisms of control and tendencies towards deviation and disjunction. Typically, role and personality theories intermingle here: whether we begin with frustration of individual needs engendering collective discontent (Fromm), or organized deviance (Parsons's 'revolutionary subculture'), the wholly unpredictable course of these disjunctive movements creates a problem, not a theory of social change. Like the old personality principle, such collective movements with their revolutionary *élan*, their unstable and volatile elements and their apparent spontaneity serve to emphasize the uncertain and the indeterminate in social life. We are supplied with

Table 9.2. Sources of Social Change: Comparative Views

PERSONALITY	ROLE AND ROLE-SET		SOCIAL SYSTEM	
Leadership	inter-action (S-R)	conflict	deviation	social movements
Collective frustration and discontent				adjustive mechanisms of control

plentiful examples from the history of modern political parties, revolutionary movements, and the new nationalisms.

As group phenomena, the significance of deviation or conflict can be defined at two main points: its incidence (i.e. its frequency is sufficient to constitute a social problem) or its politics (the basis for new programmes of social action or for organized movements). A theory of social movements makes paramount the politics of social change; such groups and movements are bearers of active, organized programmes of change – collectively, they 'make' history.

The social psychologist may see in such a theory just another 'romance' of personality and politics. But it cannot be simply dismissed. If the weight and power of great institutions were reducible to our experience of them, if they fully lent themselves to formal descriptions of role systems, tables of organization, informal groups and the like, we should be able to have a law-like social psychology. But neither the somewhat intimate view of society as a system of interactions nor its quite impersonal one as a skyscraper of roles is more than partial. Despite our abhorrence of the lacunae of social life as reflected in the large areas marked deviance, history nonetheless teaches us to attend closely to them. Thus there is reason for directing interest to the 'underside' of social life, for in the past its movements have often been the carriers of change and innovation.

Individual crisis acquires social importance only when it is removed from the sphere of the individual and is reincorporated as a 'cause', a programme, or a movement. Thus the field of social movements is of diagnostic significance. We have no way of foreseeing, however, which movements may succeed or what direction movements may take once success or partial success has been won. Consider for example the many speculations surrounding contemporary student movements. By the tradition-minded, the movements are wishfully dismissed – the rebels will age, whims will pass; by the revolution-minded, the same movements are seen as heralding major confrontations between the old and the young, power holders and the powerless, and therefore as harbingers of major change; in between are envisioned a variety of structural adjustments, administrative shifts, and formal representation of the young by and for the young. Presumably, in assessing any of these possible outcomes, the collusive weight of other institutional factors should be considered. Age crises figure importantly; new technologies and rapid change favour the young because they involve premiums on resilience and adaptation; the 'privilege' of work and the 'burdens' of leisure fall unevenly on age, sex, and ethnic groups, and unless opportunity expands with technical and occupational changes, these are bound to become competing protest groups. We might well agree that a number of changes could easily be accommodated over time without in the least indicating that they will be. If we observe that the power slogans of the young may be viewed as attempts to harmonize power with image and age ideals, we should have to add that an uncommon emphasis on youth culture has effectively disguised the stratification of youth itself. Moreover, the clear limits to the inversion of the generational order appear in the fact of age itself; someone older has first to teach the young. This fact need imply no fixed order, as it has in the past, however, and a scrambling of age ranks rather than a fixed age order might well become the rule. Skill and adaptiveness may replace seniority and age so that the 'young old' and the 'old young' (the stable and career-minded) will find a place. But this possibility hardly solves the problems of youth, nor does it touch upon the multiple sources of discontent. Like other social problems, there are not single issues but many, and we tend to ignore this fact in thinking about possible outcomes. Here, as elsewhere, there are no rules for the multiple processes we call social change. In this sense, justification for the study of social movements (political or religious, age or sex, as the case may be) cannot lie in the sphere of the practical but in theory and history. To be practical would be to test solutions. In theory, the significance of such movements derives from their nonsystem aspects. We may even regard them as 'social indicators'; but in fact, they are part of current history – revelation comes later.

Conclusions

THE importance of role theory is undeniable; its range of influence has been vast, research engendered in its name diverse and bountiful. Here we should like to consider briefly not the constant criticisms it has carried in its wake but difficulties that have arisen in the course of time.

How, for example, can we account for the divisions within the role concept that, far from diminishing, have become acute over time, so that the very problems it set out to solve are now more sharply drawn than ever? Why is the problem of personality still a problem and the question of individuality and conformity a battleground? How did it happen that role theory and analysis fed into issues its proponents had hoped to render issueless?

In part the problem was caused by the theory's practical success. Let us consider 'personality'. In theory, role was to be a truly intermediary concept, joining the individual and his society. In practice, role analysis split up the unity of person and society and further accentuated in research procedures the division of role and self, public and private, function and purpose. Once this split occurred, a host of new versions to old individualist ideas emerged. Upturned and sloganized, they were perhaps scarcely recognizable, but we may briefly examine three favourites: identity, privacy and choice. Where, sociologically speaking, the problem for modern man is anonymity, turned about and made subjective it becomes an anguished 'Who am I' and therewith gives us the psychology of identity crisis. The problems of anonymity and identity, whose social derivations were contained within various extensions of role theory, disappeared into 'ego psychology'. Sociologically, the problem of privatization is one of withdrawal and apathy, criteria of which we may find in certain measures of political and social participation. The psychic need for privacy is quite another matter on which the individual alone can speak. But privacy, as such, is always a public issue, as our freedoms are, and has nothing to do with psychology. Here, the divisions in role analysis between self and role, or public and private roles, were too easily fused with the notion of fixed boundaries that typified individualist psychologies. In role theory, privacy is not property nor are private roles something of our very own; but a confusion of terms has contributed to confusion of meaning so that private roles are scarcely distinguishable from the old 'private self'.

In a similar way, the problem of choice and volition was cast forward once again. That we speak of the social allocation of roles in itself neither restricts nor enlarges the degree of freedom of the person to choose. Moreover, the presence of choice may prove little about self-determination. One may choose an occupation to please one's self or an alter ego; both are choices, but one satisfies the nominal criterion of self-determination and one does not. In fact, matters of choice are little altered by role theory, but the spectre of social determinism looms large so that the strength of self-determination is easily ranged against it. Needless to say, as far as the question of psychological versus sociological determinism is concerned, both are highly deterministic, and the issue of moral autonomy is not an issue that divides psychology from sociology.

In short, the sociologist emphasizes those critical modern turns by which the person – differentiated, complex, the bearer of many roles – comes to feel, in his organized social experience, distanced and estranged from the great social organizations of which he was a part. In tying role analysis to the theory of bureaucratization, it would hardly occur to him to blame the person for his failure to achieve a fully rounded life or mastery of his fate.* Yet we are well aware

---

* In this connection, it is useful to remember themes that A. Gouldner examined at some length in 'Metaphysical Pathos and the Theory of Bureaucracy', reprinted in L. Coser and B. Rosenberg, *Sociological Theory*, Collier-Macmillan, 1969.

of the facility with which role analysis was rerouted. The smallness of the self or the insignificance of the individual may or may not be an everyday social experience; to compound an identity crisis, we need only range against that experience countless moral invocations to self-affirmation and autonomy.

Psychological adaptations of role theory in small groups typically run this course. Moralistic aspects shine through the cleverest of our experiments with their ready divisions between yielders and nonyielders, yea and nay sayers, conformists and deviants.* Yet to be social is to adapt and adjust and forgo the sovereignty of the ego, and the social price of resistance or individuality or autonomy is made abundantly clear in the role language of rejection, conflict and isolation. But the social price is (logically) independent of its moral value (and he who pays is the first to declare that his moral values are above price). In short, from the standpoint of role theory, roles are independent or deviant according to norms arbitrarily set, and their moral evaluation is a separate matter altogether. Whether we judge such roles to be more spontaneous or authentic belongs to another sphere of discourse.

In these confusions of doctrine, it has come about that far from settling old issues, role theory has served to dramatize them. Its proponents have had much to say about the fate of the individual in a thoroughly deindividualized world. But

---

* The vocabulary of moral individualism is well represented in the following quote from the conclusion of a notable and highly sophisticated research on social influence: 'The implications of the foregoing results are not particularly optimistic for those who place a high value on the ability of an individual to *resist* group pressures which run counter to his individual judgement. In the experimental situation we employed, the subject, by allowing himself to be *influenced* by others, in effect, *acquiesced* in the distortion of his judgement and denied the *authenticity* of his own immediate experience. The strength of the normative social influences that were generated in the course of our experiment was small; had it been stronger, one would have expected even more *distortion* and *submission*' (M. Deutsch and H. Gerard, 'A Study of Normative and Informational Social Influences Upon Individual Judgment', in Cartwright and Zander (1968). The italics have been added.

useful and influential as it may have been, role theory has often come to stand for the evil world and personality for the kingdom within you.

It is true that, for sociology, the question of personality and individuality can never lie within the person. Yet in our own time, if it is not given to us to see the person as the bearer of unique or individual values, it is nonetheless true that personal choice and identification and numerous options are expressed through group affiliations. If the individual is powerless, the group may not be. Without hastening on to the apotheosis of the group – for it should be transparently clear that both the individual and the group are still with us – we should instead emphasize here some inherent limitations of social behaviourism.

We have suggested that its very practical success and adaptation came to be at variance with its original conceptions; and when social behaviourism evolved simply into behaviourism, its problems were exactly those of other behaviourists so that the controversies between various psychological schools were repeated here. In theory, Mead's correction of behaviourism was truly an idealist solution, for social behaviourism did preserve the realm of subjectivity and intention as well as the 'I' of impulse, choice, and spontaneity. In practice these disappeared, and the analysis of the 'the act' split into the old standard components (self versus role, individual versus group, psychology versus sociology).

But if we turn again to the theory, we would also have to agree that its solutions were ultimately undone by other practical social problems – problems that have become accentuated over time. That mind, self and society achieve unity only through common meanings and shared symbols does not mean that we thereby achieve conflictless unanimity. There can be no automatic guarantee of harmony between 'I' and 'me' aspects; problems of conflict, error and diversity are still with us. The capacity of the 'generalized other' to solve all is not boundless, nor is it all-absorbing. In short, we face the same impasse that proved a fatal feature of all past idealist solutions in society and politics, only more so.

Role theory appears to have a remarkable specificity for our time, of course, for its formulations have come to be routine replications of the social order. Hence its original truth proved, to many, a daily sorrow. As an offshoot of American pragmatism, it was converted into social psychology and a kind of 'sociology of the mind'. It plausibly related us to others in our immediate environment ('significant others') and idealistically extended this into a greeting to the world (the 'generalized other'). But if, in reality, man is not emancipated from his specialized role and position and perspective, if instead he is bound over to narrow and exclusive perspectives and interests, the 'rule of roles' becomes simply an arbitrary and confining rule.*

From role conceptions it is possible to derive a self – pluralist, diversified, social – whose complexity derives not from depth or hiddenness or secrecy but from variety and contrast and multiplicity. But this self requires conditions of openness, freedom, and broad participation (so Mead visualized it). If, instead, its principles are invoked in a social world marked by the closure of increasing specialization, sharply defined statuses and positions, competing rules and norms, both self and society appear destined for an incessant round of conflict. Amidst a multitude of claims and counterclaims, ideas of harmony and equilibrium sound hollow. The idea of unitary, systemic functioning in which the relation between individual and society is viewed as essentially harmonious because 'each needs and contributes to the needs of the other' is belied by a series of social changes that either 'island' whole groups or threaten the very concept of stable role structure.

* Hence, of course, it is to be questioned by those who felt confined by it. The long counter-sociological critique has included the following elements: those niches in social life called roles, are they not just man reflecting the division of labour in society, bureaucratized, organization man? Is not man as a role-taking, role-playing creature – theatrical man – the embodiment not of the credible but the incredible in social life? As for 'filling roles', if we are no more (and often considerably less) than the fulfilment of others' expectations, is not that 'alien self' just what is asked for today?

Today when blocs, groups and subcultures emerge like islands in a social sea, the edifice of roles appears wholly vulnerable to attack. In sociology this vulnerability appeared first as dissatisfaction with a theory too devoted to system and too inattentive to its conflicts and its crises. In psychology and politics it appeared in declarations of boldness and of egoism, of self-reliance and individuality.

We may believe in the determined nature of social events and still not acquiesce to their inevitability or unalterability but to their manageability within or assailability from without. The passivity into which role analysis came to be cast as a 'system' was effectively challenged not in theory and criticism but by the actual course of 'disorderly' events. Similarly, the timeliness and relevance of role analysis will appear to have exhausted itself not, we suspect, because its research reaches an impasse, but because society itself changes. Is there reason to anticipate a time when man's social and psychic existence cannot be summarized in terms of roles?

Only counter-utopias have thus far been envisioned. Historically, the sociology of roles has developed in the context of specialization, technicization and bureaucracy. Sometimes, therefore, it has been suggested that technological evolution alone will destroy the social world of roles; machines will abolish roles or so standardize those that remain that no meaningful connections can be drawn for social psychology. More commonly, it has been predicted that increasing specialization and narrowing of roles will be accompanied by a freezing of status so that the concept would appear no longer useful or illuminating. Only technical problems would remain.

The 'super ant-hill' is old and yet modern. Like H. G. Wells's *First Men in the Moon* (1901):

. . . every citizen knows his place. He is born to that place and the elaborate discipline of training and education and surgery he undergoes fits him at last so completely to it that he has neither ideas nor organs for any purpose beyond it. 'Why should he?' Phi-oo would ask. If, for example, a Selenite is destined to be a mathematician, his teachers and trainers set out at once to that end. They check any incipient disposition to other pursuits, they encourage his mathematical bias with a perfect psychological skill. His brain grows, or at least the mathematical faculties of his brain grow, and the rest of him only so much as is necessary to sustain this essential part of him [p. 222].

On all sides, the 'technological society' has long been viewed as driven to extremes of specialization and closure. In its evolution, the wedding of social and psychological types makes many roles fixed and absolute. Some even see in this rigidity a harmoniously managed society – harmonious because it is thoroughly specialized, inside and out. In that event, role is stillborn.

The concept itself is vital so long as it is vitalized, i.e. so long as it implies margins of flexibility, choice, and many-sidedness. It is possible to emphasize its formal, impersonal and technocratic aspects – its marvellous 'fit' with technological society. When that happens, when the ancient meaning of role as a living function or an 'enactment' is forgone, our social psychology will also appear exhausted. It will have lost its capacity to interest us in roles as living functions – as the human aspect of the division of labour in society.

Appendix

A chronology of social psychologies and social-psychological researches centrally related to the text

DATE	THEORY OR TEXT	DATE	RESEARCH
1890–1900			
1890	W. James: *Principles of Psychology* (the many-selved self)		
1893	Durkheim: *Division of Labor* (forms of solidarity and definition of *'conscience collective'*)		
1895	Le Bon: *The Crowd* ('crowd mind')		
1900–1910			
1908	W. McDougall: *Social Psychology*		

185

APPENDIX

DATE	THEORY OR TEXT	DATE	RESEARCH
	E. A. Ross: *Social Psychology*		
1910	G. Simmel: 'Fundamental Problems of Sociology' (the individual and society); 'The Forms of Sociology' (interaction process)		
	Lévy-Bruhl: *Les Fonctions mentales dans les sociétés inférieures* (ethno-psychology)		
1910–20			
1920	W. McDougall: *Group Mind*	1920	F. Allport: the influence of the group on individual performance
1920–30			
1921	S. Freud: *Group Psychology and the Analysis of the Ego*		

DATE	THEORY OR TEXT	DATE	RESEARCH
1929	B. Malinowski: *Sexual Life of Savages* (ethnology versus psychoanalysis)		
1930	G. H. Mead: *Mind, Self and Society*, published posthumously (social behaviourism)		
1930–40			
		1936	M. Sherif: *Psychology of Social Norms*
		1939	Lewin, Lippitt and White: experimental group 'climates'
1940–50			
1941	E. Fromm: *Fear of Freedom* (the anal-sadistic character and authoritarianism)		

DATE	THEORY OR TEXT	DATE	RESEARCH
1942	M. Mead on America, G. Gorer on Japan, Dicks on Germany, *et al.* (social character becomes national character and vice versa)		
		1943	W. Wolff: experiments in self-recognition
		1947	A. Davis and R. Havighurst: *Father of the Man* (the socialization debate gets under way)
1950–60			
1950	T. Parsons: *The Social System* (role theory is 'systematized')	1950	T. Adorno *et al.*: *The Authoritarian Personality*
	E. Erikson: *Childhood and Society* (identity becomes a psychological problem)		R. Bales: interaction process analysis

DATE 1950	THEORY OR TEXT	DATE	RESEARCH
	D. Riesman *et al.*: *Lonely Crowd* (other-direction and peer-group dominance)		
		1952	S. Asch: *Social Psychology* (summary of research on individual 'independence' or 'submission' to group influence)
		1953	I. Hovland *et al.*: the 'unpersuasible person' in opinion research
		1954	Inkeles and Levinson: national character as 'modal personality'
1956	W. H. Whyte: *Organization Man* (group togetherness and conformity)		
1959	E. Goffman: *The Presentation of Self* (drama-turgy of inter-action process)		

Bibliography

Adorno, T., E. Fraenkel-Brunswick *et al.*, *The Authoritarian Personality*, London: Harper & Row, 1950.

Allport, F., *Social Psychology*, Cambridge, Mass.: Houghton & Mifflin, 1924.

Allport, G., *Personality*, London: Constable, 1937.

— *The Nature of Prejudice*, London: Addison-Wesley, 1954.

Archer, W., *Masks or Faces?* Longmans Green, 1888.

Aries, P., *Centuries of Childhood*, Jonathan Cape, 1962.

Asch, S., *Social Psychology*, Englewood Cliffs, N.J.: Prentice-Hall, 1952.

Baker, E. F., *Technology and Women's Work*, London: Columbia University Press, 1965.

Bales, R., *Interaction Process Analysis*, Cambridge, Mass.: Addison-Wesley, 1950.

Banton, M., *Roles*, Tavistock Press, 1965.

Bauer, R., *The New Man in Soviet Psychology*, Oxford University Press, 1952.

Bauer, R., *et al.*, *Second Order Consequences*, London: MIT Press, 1969.

Berger, M., T. Abel and C. Page, *Freedom and Control in Modern Society*, New York: D. van Nostrand, 1954.

Berger, P., and T. Luckmann, *The Social Construction of Reality*, Allen Lane The Penguin Press, 1967.

Berkowitz, L., 'Personality and Group Position', *Sociometry*, 1956, 19, pp. 210–22.

Bettelheim, B., and M. Janowitz, *Social Change and Prejudice*, Collier-Macmillan, 1964.

Biddle, B., and E. Thomas, *Role Theory*, London: J. Wiley, 1966.

Borgatta, E., 'Role Playing Specification, Personality, and Performance', *Sociometry*, 1961, 24, pp. 218–33.

— 'A Note on the Consistency of Subject Behavior in

Interaction Process Analysis', *Sociometry*, 1964, 27, pp. 222–6.

Borgatta, E., T. Couch and R. Bales, 'Some Findings Relevant to the Great Man Theory of Leadership', in Borgatta, Bales, and Hare, *Small Groups*, New York: A. Knopf, 1955.

Boring, E., *A History of Experimental Psychology*, New York: Century, 1929.

Brim, O., and S. Wheeler, *Socialization after Childhood*, London: J. Wiley, 1966.

Bronfenbrenner, U., 'The Changing American Child', *Journal of Social Issues*, 1961, 17, pp. 6–18.

Buchanan, W., and H. Cantril, *How Nations See Each Other*, Urbana: University of Illinois Press, 1953.

Butler, S., *The Way of All Flesh*, Longman, 1966.

Campbell, D., and R. LaVine, 'Cross-cultural Research on Ethnocentrism', *Journal of Conflict Resolution*, 1961, 5, pp. 82–108.

Cartwright, D., and A. Zander, *Group Dynamics*, Tavistock, 1968.

Clausen, J. (ed.), *Socialization and Society*, Boston: Little, Brown, 1968.

Couch, C., 'Self Attitudes and Degree of Agreement with Immediate Others', *American Journal of Sociology*, 1958, 63, pp. 491–6.

Crutchfield, R., 'Conformity and Character', reprinted in E. Hollander and R. Hunt, *Current Perspectives in Social Psychology*, New York: Oxford University Press, 1963.

Dahrendorf, R., 'Homo Sociologicus', *Essays in the Theory of Society*, Stanford: Stanford University Press, 1968.

Deutsch, M., 'Trust and Suspicion', *Journal of Conflict Resolution*, 1958, 2, pp. 265–79.

Dicks, H. V., 'German Personality Traits and National Socialist Ideology', *Human Relations*, 1950, 3, pp. 111–54.

Duijker, H. J., and N. Frijda, *National Character and National Stereotypes*, Amsterdam: N. Holland Publishing Co., 1960.

Durkheim, E., *The Elementary Forms of Religious Life*, Allen & Unwin, 1915.

Embree, J., 'Standard Error and Japanese Character', *World Politics*, 1950, 2, pp. 439–43.

Emmett, D., *Rules, Roles and Relations*, New York: St Martin's Press, 1966.

Erikson, E., *Childhood and Society*, Hogarth Press, 1964.

Freud, S., *Group Psychology and the Analysis of the Ego*, New York: Bantam, 1960.

Fromm, E., *Fear of Freedom*, Routledge & Kegan Paul, 1942.

Gallie, W. B., *Peirce and Pragmatism*, Constable, 1966.

Gerth, H., and C. W. Mills, *Character and Social Structure*, Routledge & Kegan Paul, 1954.

Gilbert, G., 'Stereotype Persistence and Change among College Students', *Journal of Abnormal and Social Psychology*, 1951, 46, pp. 245–54.

Goffman, E., *The Presentation of Self in Everyday Life*, Allen Lane The Penguin Press, 1969.

— *Encounters*, Allen Lane The Penguin Press, 1972.

Goode, W., 'Theory of Role Strain', *American Sociological Review*, 1960, 25, pp. 483–96.

Gorer, G., and J. Rickman, *People of Great Russia*, Cresset Press, 1949.

Green, A., 'The Middle Class Male Child and Neurosis', reprinted in R. Bendix and S. Lipset, *Class, Status and Power*, New York: Free Press, 1953.

Grey, A. (ed.), *Class and Personality in Society*, New York: Atherton, 1969.

Hare, P., *Handbook of Small Group Research*, New York: Free Press, 1962.

Hare, P., E. Borgatta and R. Bales (eds.), *Small Groups*, New York: A. Knopf, 1955.

Hartmann, H., E. Kris and R. Lowenstein, 'Some Psychoanalytic Comments on Culture and Personality', in G. B. Wilbur and W. Muensterberger (eds.), *Psychoanalysis and Culture*, New York: International Universities Press, 1951.

Haythorn, W., 'Influence of Individual Members on the

Characteristics of Small Groups', in Hare, Borgatta and Bales, *Small Groups*, New York: A. Knopf, 1955.

Haythorn, W., and A. Crouch, 'The Behavior of Authoritarian and Equalitarian Personalities in Small Groups', *Human Relations*, 1956, 9, pp. 57–94.

Heberle, R., *Social Movements – An Introduction to Political Sociology*, New York: Appleton Century, 1951.

Hollander, E., and R. Hunt, *Current Perspectives in Social Psychology*, New York: Oxford University Press, 1963.

Horton, J., 'The Dehumanization of Anomie and Alienation', *British Journal of Sociology*, 1964, 15, pp. 283–300.

Hovland, C., I. Janis and H. Kelley, *Communication and Persuasion*, London: Yale University Press, 1953.

Hsu, F. L. K. (ed.), *Psychological Anthropology*, Homewood: Dorsey Press, 1961.

Inkeles, A., and K. Geiger, *Soviet Society*, Constable, 1961.

Inkeles, A., and D. Levinson, 'National Character: The Study of Modal Personality and Socio-cultural Systems', in G. Lindzey, *Handbook of Social Psychology*, vol. 2, London: Addison-Wesley, 1969.

James, W., *Principles of Psychology*, Dover/Constable, 1958.

Jourard, S., *The Transparent Self*, London: D. van Nostrand, 1964.

Joyce, J., *Ulysses*, Bodley Head, 1960.

Kahn, R., *et al.*, *Organizational Stress*, London: J. Wiley, 1964.

Karpf, F., *American Social Psychology*, New York: McGraw-Hill, 1932.

Katz, E., and P. Lazarsfeld, *Personal Influence*, New York: Free Press, 1955.

Kirscht, J. P., and R. C. Dillehay, *Dimensions of Authoritarianism*, Lexington: University of Kentucky Press, 1967.

Klein, V., *The Feminine Character*, New York: International Universities Press, 1949.

Klineberg, O., and R. Christie, *Perspectives in Social Psychology*, London: Holt, Rinehart & Winston, 1965.

Kluckhohn, C., 'Studies of Russian National Character', in A. Inkeles and K. Geiger, *Soviet Society*, Constable, 1961.

Koestler, A., *Darkness at Noon*, Jonathan Cape, 1940.

Kuhn, M., 'Self Attitudes by Age, Sex and Professional Training', *Sociological Quarterly*, 1960, 1, pp. 39–55.

Kuhn, M., and T. McPartland, 'An Empirical Investigation of Self Attitudes', *American Sociological Review*, 1954, 19, pp. 68–78.

Lambert, W. W., and W. E. Lambert, *Social Psychology*, London: Prentice-Hall, 1964.

Lang, K., and G. Lang, *Collective Dynamics*, New York: Crowell Co., 1961.

Lazarsfeld, P., and R. Merton, 'Friendship as a Social Process', in M. Berger *et al.*, *Freedom and Control in Modern Society*, New York: D. van Nostrand, 1954.

Le Bon, G., *The Crowd*, London: T. Fisher Unwin, 1897.

Levinger, G., 'Task and Social Behavior in Marriage', *Sociometry*, 1964, 27, pp. 433–48.

Levinson, D., 'Role, Personality and Social Structure', in L. Coser and B. Rosenberg, *Sociological Theory*, Collier-Macmillan, 1969.

Lévy-Bruhl, L., *Primitive Mentality*, New York, Macmillan, 1923.

Lewin, K., R. Lippitt and R. White, 'Patterns of Behavior in Experimentally Created Social Climates', *Journal of Social Psychology*, 1939, X, pp. 271–99.

Lieberman, S., 'Effects of Change in Roles on the Attitudes of Role Occupants', *Human Relations*, 1956, 9, pp. 385–402.

Lindesmith, A., and A. Strauss, 'Critique of Culture and Personality Writings', *American Sociological Review*, 1958, 36, pp. 297–303.

Lipset, S., and L. Lowenthal, *Culture and Social Character*, New York: Free Press, 1961.

McClelland, D., *Roots of Consciousness*, New York: D. van Nostrand, 1964.

McDougall, W., *Social Psychology*, Boston: J. Luce, 1923.

— *Group Mind*, New York: G. P. Putnam, 1920.

McGranahan, D., 'A Comparison of Social Attitudes among American and German Youth', *Journal of Abnormal and Social Psychology*, 1946, 41, pp. 245–57.

McGrath, J., and I. Altman, *Small Group Research*, New York: Holt, Rinehart & Winston, 1966.

Mann, T., *Confessions of Felix Krull, Confidence Man*, Secker & Warburg, 1955.

Mead, G. H., *Mind, Self and Society*, London: University of Chicago Press, 1968.

Mead, M., *Soviet Attitudes Toward Authority*, New York: McGraw-Hill, 1951.

— (ed.), *Cultural Patterns and Technological Change*, New York: Mentor Books, 1955.

Meenes, M., 'Comparison of Racial Stereotypes, 1935 and 1942', *Journal of Social Psychology*, 1947, 17, pp. 327–36.

Merton, R., 'Social Structure and Anomie', *Social Theory and Social Structure*, New York: Free Press, 1957.

— 'The Role-Set', in L. Coser and B. Rosenberg, *Sociological Theory*, Collier-Macmillan, 1969.

Milgram, S., 'Nationality and Conformity', *Scientific American*, December 1961, pp. 45–51.

Miller, D., and G. Swanson, *Inner Conflict and Defense*, Folkestone: Bailey Bros & Swinfen, 1968.

Mishler, E., 'Personality Characteristics and the Resolution of Role Conflict', *Public Opinion Quarterly*, 1953, 17, pp. 115–35.

Miyamoto, S., and S. Dornbusch, 'Test of Interactionist Hypothesis of Self Conception', *American Journal of Sociology*, 1956, 61, pp. 399–403.

Moment, D., and A. Zaleznik, *Role Development and Interpersonal Competence*, Folkestone: Bailey Bros & Swinfen, 1963.

Moore, C. A. (ed.), *The Status of the Individual in East and West*, Honolulu: University of Hawaii Press, 1968.

Moore, W. E., *Social Change*, London: Prentice-Hall, 1967.

Newcomb, T., R. Turner and P. Converse, *Social Psychology*, New York: Holt, Rinehart & Winston, 1960.

Niehoff, A., *A Casebook of Social Change*, London: Aldine, 1966.

Ogburn, W., and S. Gilfillan, 'Inventions', *Recent Social Trends*, New York: McGraw-Hill, 1933.

Orlansky, H., 'Infant Care and Personality', *Psychological Bulletin*, 1949, 46, pp. 1–48.

Pappenheim, F., *Alienation of Modern Man*, London: Monthly Review Press, 1959.

Parsons, T., *The Social System*, Routledge & Kegan Paul, 1952.

Parsons, T., R. Bales *et al.*, *Family: Socialization and Interaction Process*, Routledge & Kegan Paul, 1956.

Patai, R. (ed.), *Women in the Modern World*, Collier-Macmillan, 1967.

Pettigrew, T. F., 'Personality and Socio-cultural Factors in Intergroup Attitudes', *Journal of Conflict Resolution*, 1958, 2, pp. 29–42.

Regamey, D., 'The Individual and the Universal in East and West', in Moore, *The Status of the Individual in East and West*.

Reischauer, E., *The United States and Japan*, Oxford University Press, 1965.

Rudé, G., *The Crowd in History*, London: J. Wiley, 1965.

Saksena, S. K., 'The Individual in Social Thought and Practice in India', in Moore, *The Status of the Individual in East and West*.

Seago, D., 'Stereotypes Before Pearl Harbor and After', *Journal of Psychology*, 1947, 23, pp. 55–63.

Secord, P. F., and C. W. Backman, *Social Psychology*, London: McGraw-Hill, 1964.

Sewell, W., 'Infant Training and the Personality of the Child', *American Journal of Sociology*, 1952, 58, pp. 150–59.

— 'Some Recent Developments in Socialization Theory and Research', *Annals of the American Academy of Political and Social Science*, 1963, 349, pp. 163–81.

Sherif, M., *Outline of Social Psychology*, London: Harper & Row, 1956.

Sherif, M., and M. Wilson (eds.), *Group Relations at the Crossroads*, New York: Harper & Row, 1953.

Shibutani, T., *Society and Personality*, Englewood Cliffs, N.J.: Prentice-Hall, 1961.

Simmel, E., R. Hoppe and G. Milton, *Social Facilitation and Imitative Behavior*, Boston: Allyn & Bacon, 1968.

Simmel, G., *Sociology*, Collier-Macmillan, 1950.

Slater, P., 'Parental Role Differentiation', *American Journal of Sociology*, 1961, 67, pp. 296–308.

Smelser, N., *Theory of Collective Behaviour*, Routledge & Kegan Paul, 1962.

Smith, D., 'Modal Attitude Clusters', *Social Forces*, 1966, 44, pp. 526–8.

Solomon, L., 'Influence of Types of Power Relationships and Game Strategies upon the Development of Interpersonal Trust', *Journal of Abnormal and Social Psychology*, 1960, 61, pp. 223–30.

Sorokin, P., and C. Berger, *Time Budgets of Human Behavior*, Cambridge, Mass.: Harvard University Press, 1939.

Steiner, I., and H. Johnson, 'Authoritarianism and Conformity', *Sociometry*, 1963, 26, pp. 21–34.

Stock, D., and H. Thelen, *Emotional Dynamics and Group Culture*, Washington: National Training Laboratories, 1958.

Stoetzel, J., 'G. Le Bon', in *International Encyclopedia of Social Science*, 9, New York: Macmillan, 1968.

Stouffer, S., and J. Toby, 'Role Conflict and Personality', *American Journal of Sociology*, 1951, 56, pp. 395–406.

Tagiuri, E., and L. Patrullo, *Person, Perception and Interpersonal Behavior*, Stanford: Stanford University Press, 1958.

Thackeray, W., *Vanity Fair*, Glasgow: Blackie, 1958.

Toch, H., *Social Psychology of Social Movements*, Methuen, 1966.

Tuckman, B., 'Personality Structure, Group Composition and Group Functioning', *Sociometry*, 1964, 27, pp. 469–82.

Ullmann, W., *The Individual and Society in the Middle Ages*, Baltimore: Johns Hopkins Press, 1966.

Verba, S., *Small Groups and Political Behavior*, Princeton: Princeton University Press, 1961.

Walker, E., and R. Heyns, *An Anatomy for Conformity*, Englewood Cliffs, N.J.: Prentice-Hall, 1962.

Wells, H. G., *First Men in the Moon*, Unwin, 1925.

Wepman, J., and R. Heine, *Concepts of Personality*, Chicago: Aldine, 1963.

Wilensky, J., and H. Edwards, 'The Skidder: Ideological Adjustments of Downward Mobile Workers', *American Sociological Review*, 1959, 64, pp. 215–31.

Willer, D., *Scientific Sociology*, London: Prentice-Hall, 1967.

Willis, R., 'Conformity, Independence and Anti-conformity', *Human Relations*, 1965, 18, pp. 373–87.

Wolff, W., *The Expression of Personality*, New York: Harper & Row, 1943.

Yinger, M., *Toward a Field Theory of Behaviour*, London: McGraw-Hill, 1965.

Yinger, M., and G. Simpson, *Racial and Cultural Minorities*, New York: Harper & Row, 1958.

Index

achievement motivation, 70, 129, 159
actor, 49–50, 54, 55–56
age roles, 33, 176–77
alienation, 30, 31
Allport, F., 17–19, 20, 21–22, 23
anomie, xiii, 30, 31, 144
anthropology (influence on socialization theory), 67–68
Aries, P., 67n
Asch, S., 19–20, 24, 25
authoritarian personality, 21, 25, 26, 100–101, 107, 123–26
autonomy, 26
of the social, 11–12, 51

balance theory, 102–104
Bales, R., 89–90, 91, 98, 99
Bauer, R., 85n, 157
Bavelas, A., and H. Leavitt, 166
behaviourism, xiii–xiv, 46–47, 67, 84, 134–35, 181
Berger, P., and T. Luckmann, 77
Berkowitz, L., 129
Bernstein, B., 73–74
Bion, W. R., 89, 90–91
Borgatta, E., 94, 98
Brim, O., 77
Bronfenbrenner, U., 71
Buchanan, W. and H. Cantril, 117

bureaucratization, 173, 179, 183–84
Butler, S., 41–42

character, 39–40, 43–45, 107–108
feminine, 108–15
national, 115–23
social, 31, 44–45
types, 26–27
childhood, 67, 69
collective behaviour, 3–4
collective representations, 12–13
conformity, 11, 20–21, 25, 26, 30, 34–35, 144
crowd, 5–7
mind, 4–8, 12–14
psychology, 3, 5, 7
conscience collective, 11, 15
consciousness (and society), 44
Crutchfield, R., 20–21, 25

Davis, A., and R. Havighurst, 70
Dahrendorf, R., 34n, 143
deception, 56–7
delinquent personality, 126–28
Deutsch, M., and H. Gerard, 24, 180n
deviance, 127–28, 149, 168–69, 175, 176
disclosure, 85–86

dramaturgical theory, 51–60
Durkheim, E., xiii, 11–12, 30

ego psychology, 83, 178
élites, 122, 123
Emmet, D., 147n
exchange theory, 103, 146
externalization (of social act),
    88–89

formal sociology, 49, 51
Freud, S., 7, 67, 68–69
    Freudian theory, 10, 45–46,
    68–70, 71, 81, 119
Fromm, E., 31n, 79, 100n

generalized other, 61, 72, 75,
    76, 81, 135, 181
Gerth, H., and C. W. Mills, 62,
    81, 83, 149n
Goffman, E., xvi, 49–51, 56–57,
    84, 135, 140, 146
Goode, W., 170n
Gorer, G., 118
Gouldner, A., 179n
Green, A., 71
group, 15
    frame of reference, 23–24,
    25, 27, 29
    influence of, 9, 16–19, 21–24,
    27
    mind, 12–15
    personality, 94–96
    psychology, xviii, 7

Hare, P., 94
Haythorn, W., 95, 98n
'homo sociologicus', 143
Hovland, C., I. Janis and
    H. Kelley, 25
Hyman, H., 104

identity crisis, 141–42, 178
individual, xi–xiii, 15
    historical types, 121–22, 131
    psychology, 5, 44
individualization, 79–82
Inkeles, A., and D. Levinson,
    119
instincts, 10
instrumental and emotional
    acts, 90–91
interaction, 11, 28, 103
    process analysis, 89
    theory, xvii, 32–36, 84
internalization, 47, 72–74, 76
intimacy, 101–107
introspection, xv, 137–38

James, W., 9, 10, 45
Jourard, S., 85
Joyce, J., 42–43

Kahn, R., 169
Katz, E., and P. Lazarsfeld,
    29n
Kluckhohn, C., 119
Koestler, A., 85

laboratory culture, 8, 92
Lambert, W. W. and
    W. E. Lambert, 25
Lang, K., and G. Lang, 3, 7
Lazarsfeld, P., and R. Merton,
    105
leadership, 50, 91, 97–101, 159
Le Bon, G., 5–7, 13–14
Lévi-Strauss, C., 80
Lévy-Bruhl, L., 13–14, 80
Lewin, K., R. Lippitt and
    R. White, 96
Lieberman, S., 166

McDougall, W., 10, 12–15
McGranahan, D., 120
McGrath, J., and I. Altman, 95n, 96n
Malinowski, B., 69
Mann, T., 57–58
Marx, K., 30
mass psychology, 29
Mead, G. H., 32, 46–49, 61, 67, 72, 76, 81, 83, 87–88, 135, 149, 181
Mead, M., 116n, 118, 172
Merton, R., xiii, 140, 144
Milgram, S., 120
Mill, J. S., 114
Miller, D., and G. Swanson, 73
mind, 44
minorities, 35
Miyamoto, S., and S. Dornbusch, 88
mobility, 54–55, 57, 59, 110, 113
modal personality, 119
modernization, 44, 153–54
Moment, D., and A. Zaleznik, 62
Moore, W. E., 154
motivation theory, 144, 148–49

nationalism, 172–73
Newcomb, T., 104
norm, convergence on, 17, 19, 27–28
novel, 39–43

Ogburn, W. F., and S. Gilfillan, 155
organization man, 30
Orlansky, H., 71
Orwell, G., 85

paradox of acting, 55–56
Parsons, T., 35n, 62, 84, 99, 142, 144, 166, 167
Peirce, C. S., 82–83
person, xi–xii, xiv
  boundaries, xvi, 59
  empirical, xv
personal influence, 28–29
personality, xii–xiv, xv–xvi, 45–48, 55, 59, 78
  and social change, 159–65
  politics of, 74–75
  problem of, xvii
  relation to authoritarian attitudes, 123–24
  small groups and, 92–97
  see also authoritarian personality; delinquent personality
persuasibility experiments, 25
Piaget, J., 67
planning, 170–71, 173
prejudice, 117–18, 125
privacy, 56, 106–107, 139, 178–79
psychoanalytic personality theory, 45–46, 84, 118–19

reciprocity rule, 103, 146
role theory, 32–34, 48–51, 87–89, 131–32
  and theatre, 52–54
  conflict, 167–70
  distance, 59, 140, 146
  multiplicity, 41, 59, 146–47
  reversal, 140
  specialization, 91, 96–97, 97–98
Ross, E. A., 6
Rudé, G., 3

Sears, R., E. Maccoby and H. Levin, 70
second-order effects, 157
Secord, P., and C. Backman, 22, 137
self, xvii, 45–46, 48, 133
  and social structure, 80–83
  boundaries, xvi
  conception, East and West, 87
  fragmented, 89, 139–40
  image, 83–84, 88, 137–38
  measures of, 136
  transparent, 85
Sewell, W., 71, 76n
sex roles, 34, 108–109, 112–13
Sherif, M., 17, 19, 20, 23–24, 28, 29n
Simmel, G., 49, 102, 140
small group, 92–93
small scale change, 171–72
Smelser, N., 3, 7
social behaviourism, xvii, 32, 46–47, 84, 85, 87–90, 138, 181
social change, 125–26, 153–65
social class, 69–74
social facilitation, 17–18, 21–22
socialization theory, 67–68
  and life cycle, 75–76
  primary and secondary, 69–74
social movements, 175–77
social perception, 19, 138
social system, 84, 170
sociometry, 97, 103, 104

stereotypes, 116–19
Stock, D., and H. Thelen, 89, 90, 91
structural effects, 111–12, 164–65
superego, 69, 70, 73, 74, 75
survey research, 120–21

Tarde, G., 6, 13
task and emotional specialists, 90–91, 101
team analysis, 50, 146
Thackeray, W., 40–41
traits, 128–32
trust and suspicion, 132
Tuckman, B., 95

Ullmann, W., 81, 82
unconscious, 7
  self evaluation, 138

Van Gennep, A., 166
Verba, S., 99

Walker, E., and R. Heyns, 22, 25
Weber, M., 28n
Wells, H. G., 183–84
Whyte, W. H., 30, 55, 103
Woolf, W., 137–38
women, 108–15

Yinger, M., and G. Simpson, 125
youth, 177